I0160084

Word Building Activities

for beginners of English

Susan Boyer

Boyer Educational Resources 2009
Reprinted 2011,2018

Published by
Boyer Educational Resources
for worldwide distribution.

Phone/fax +61 2 4739 1538
Web address: www.boyereducation.com.au

Acknowledgments

I would like to express my thanks to the following people for their contribution to the final presentation of this book:

Firstly, I would like to thank the teachers who trialed material in this book and suggested improvements.In particular, I wish to thank Kim Alexander, Marie Maguire and Maria Muronie for their time and constructive feedback regarding the material proposed for this book. Also, I would like to thank Maria Reid and Dianne Bernoth for their feedback on the general content and layout of the book. I would like to thank Jeanette Christian for her proofreading and editing skills. Also, I would like to thank my dear husband, Len, for his encouragement and support throughout the project. And, as always, I am indebted to the many students who have given me the necessary insight into the language needs of English language learners around the world.

The following images used herein were obtained from IMSI's MasterClips Collection, 1895 Francisco Blvd. East, San Rafael, CA 94901-5506, USA: page 44 (1,3,4,5,6), 45 (1,2,3,5,8), 62 98), 64 (2,3,4,5,6) 102 &103 (1, 9). Images on page 46 (2,3,5,6,7) where obtained from Greenstreet software Ltd. Other clip art images were obtained from Microsoft's clip Gallery, Microsoft Pty Ltd. Illustrations page 34 (6, 9) by Matthew Larwood. Other illustrations created by Susan Boyer.

Boyer, Susan
Word Building Activities for beginners of English
ISBN 978 1 877074 28 8

8th Print 2018

Boyer Educational Resources
PO Box 255, Glenbrook, 2773 Australia,
Phone/Fax +61 2 4739 1538
www.boyereducation.com.au
www.englishebooks.com - for download of eBooks (PDF) & eAudio (MP3) versions of our resources.

To the Teacher

As the name implies, *Word Building Activities for beginners of English* has been designed and developed to provide simple reference material for students at the beginner level of English language learning.

This resource can be used as foundation material to establish a repertoire of words and simple sentences from which beginner students can build and extend their knowledge. Many of the pages provide worksheets where students are actively involved in matching words to pictures. In contrast to a picture dictionary, where the words and pictures are already labelled, using this resource aids consolidation of meaning as students write the words themselves. In addition to creating accessible reference material, this process develops writing and spelling skills and raises confidence as the stock of words and phrases increases.

This book also provides **complementary material** for the student workbook **English Language Skills - Level 1** (Boyer Educational Resources, 2009). As the activities in this book follow the same topics as the units in English Language Skills - Level 1, they can be used to introduce or revise lessons.

Additionally, where low level classes have students with varying abilities, the activities in this book can be used with students who need more and simpler language building practice.

The material has been designed to be used in a classroom with teacher support. However, answers are provided at the back of the book to enable individual, self-paced activities if preferred.

Contents

Contents

Numbers and words

Write the words that spell the numbers.

1 one ______	2 two ______	3 three ______	4 four ______	5 five ______
6 six ______	7 seven ______	8 eight ______	9 nine ______	10 ten ______
11 eleven ______	12 twelve ______	13 thirteen ______	14 fourteen ______	15 fifteen ______
16 sixteen ______	17 seventeen ______	18 eighteen ______	19 nineteen ______	20 twenty ______

Using numbers

We use numbers to count 'how many' people or things. How many people are in your classroom? ___________

Ordinal numbers and words

See the people standing in a queue. We use ordinal numbers to say where people are in a queue.

Say the ordinal numbers after your teacher.

1st first, 2nd second, 3rd third, 4th fourth, 5th fifth, 6th sixth, 7th seventh, 8th eighth, 9th ninth, 10th tenth, 11th eleventh

12th twelfth, 13th thirteenth, 14th fourteenth, 15th fifteenth, 16th sixteenth, 17th seventeenth, 18th eighteenth, 19th nineteenth, 20th twentieth

We use ordinal numbers to say **the date** of each day in a month.

What is the date today? ____________________

English letters

There are 26 **letters** used to write English words.

Write the letters.

a b c d e f g h i j k l m n o p q r s t u v w x y z

a __

Capital letters

Write the letters.

A B C D E F G H I J K L M N O P Q R S T U V W X Y Z

A __

Names of people and countries start with a **capital letter**.

See the first letter of the name is a capital → Susan, Liverpool

Write your name: ____________________ Write your country: ____________________

English letters and words

Listen to your teacher and **say** the names of the letters and words beginning with the letters.

a for apples 	**b** for beetle 	**c** for cat 	**d** for dog 	**e** for eggs 	**f** for father 	**g** for glasses 
h for hat 	**i** for insects 	**j** for jacket 	**k** for kangaroo 	**l** for letter 	**m** for money 	**n** for 
o for oranges 	**p** for people 	**q** queue 	**r** for rabbit 	**s** for sun 	**t** for tea 	**u** for umbrella 
	v for vegetables 	**w** for woman 	**x** for x-ray 	**y** for 	**z** for zoo 	

Write your name.______________________ Spell your name to another person.

English Class - Saying hello

Hello. My name is Tejinder.
Hello. My name is Ana.
Hello. My name is Kim.
Hello. My name is Jo.

Write: Hello. My name is ______________________________.

Write

Hello. My name is Mai.
______ __ ____ __ Jack.
Write your name.

Name and address

1. first name	2. surname	3. address
4. suburb	5. postcode	

Write 

My full name is David Green.

1. My _____ ____ is David.
2. My ________ is Green.

3. My ________ is 24 Long Street.

4. My ______ is Glenbrook.

5. My _________ is 2773.

Name and personal details

1. first name	2. surname	3. address	4. postcode
5. phone number	6. date of birth	7. signature	

Write 

1. ________ ______

2. ___________

3. ___________

4. ____________

5. ________

____

6. ______

__

______

7. ______________

Name and personal details

Write

My _ _ _ _ _ _ _ _ _ _ is Susan.
My _ _ _ _ _ _ _ _ is Green.
24 Long Street
3.
Susan Green
24 Long Street
Glenbrook
2773
4.
5.
04 07274380
1
2 s u r n a m e
f i r s t n a m e
3 a
4
5 e
6
7
7.
Susan Green
6

What is the street address?

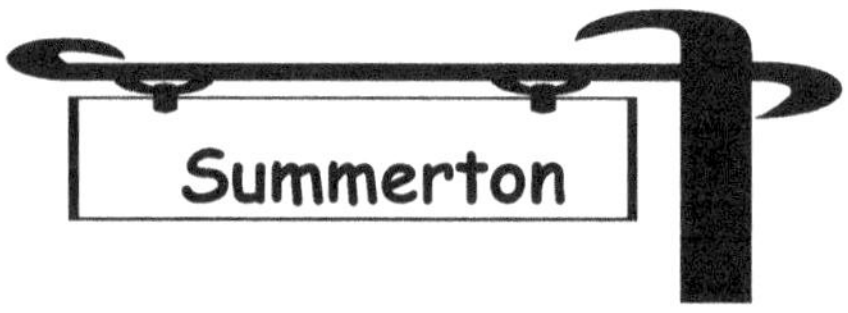

Write the street address.

1.

____

Summerton

2.

____

Summerton

3.

____

Summerton

Write your address. →

____

____

Name and address on an envelope

My address is
24 Long Street
Glenbrook

24
Long Street

Write

1. title	2. first name	3. surname	4. address
5. suburb	6. country	7. postcode	

1. ______ 2. ______ ____ 3. ________

Miss Susan Green

4. ________ → 24 Long Street

Glenbrook ← 5. _______

Australia ← 6. ________

7. _________ → 2 7 7 3

Name and address on an envelope - practise

Write the name and address of a friend.

front

Write the name here: ____________________

Write the number
and street here: ____________________

Write the suburb here: ____________________

Write the country here: ____________________

Write the postcode here: __________

Write your name and address

back

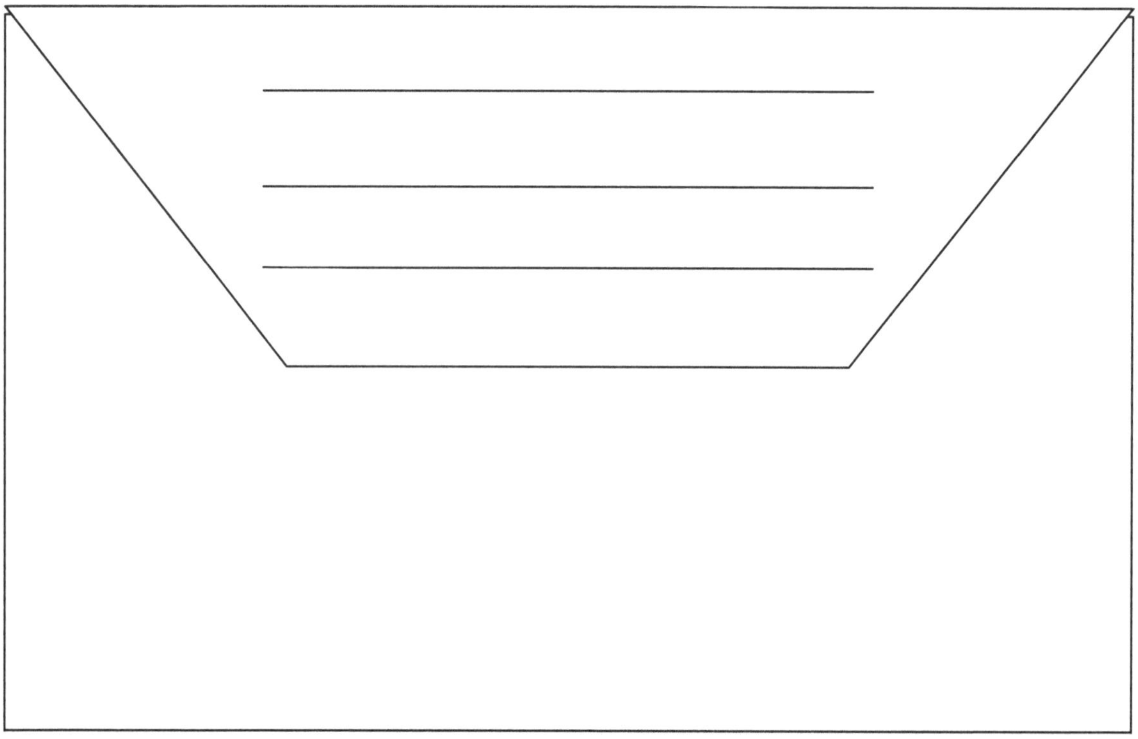

Name and address on a form 1

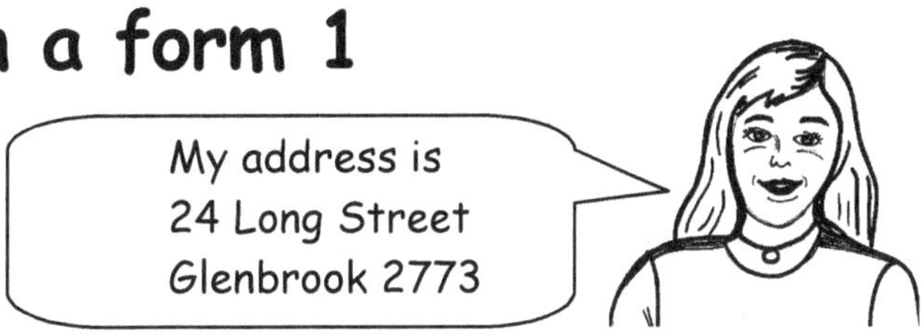
My address is
24 Long Street
Glenbrook 2773

Write about Susan Green.

Student Form	
1. First name:	2. Surname:
3. Address: ____________________ ____________________	
4. Postcode: __________	

Write about you.

Student Form	
1. First name:	2. Surname:
3. Address: ____________________ ____________________	
4. Postcode: __________	

Titles

1. Mr	2. Mrs	3. Miss	4. Ms	5. Dr

Write

1. _ _ = man (single or married)

2. _ _ _ = married woman

3. _ _ _ _ = single woman or girl

4. _ _ = a woman (single or married)

5. _ _ = man or woman doctor

Write: My title is ______________

Writing on a form

Student Form	
Title: Tick one ☑ Mr ☐ Mrs ☐ Miss ☐ Ms ☐ Dr ☐	
First name:	Surname:
Address: ______________________ ______________________ Postcode: _ _ _ _	

Name and Address on a Form 2

 Write about <u>you</u>.

Student Form	
Title: Tick ☑ Mr ☐ Mrs ☐ Miss ☐ Ms ☐ Dr ☐	
1. First name:	2. Surname:
3. Address: ______________________ ______________________ 4. Postcode: _ _ _ _	
5. Phone number:	6. Date of Birth: Date / Month / Year
7. Signature:	

What can you do now?

Put a tick ☑ next to things you can do.

I can write my name. ☐

I can write my address. ☐

I can write my phone number. ☐

I can write my date of birth. ☐

I can write my signature. ☐

Things in the classroom

1. scissors	2. pencils	3. rubber
4. highlighter	5. ruler	6. pens
7. chair and desk	8. folder	

Write

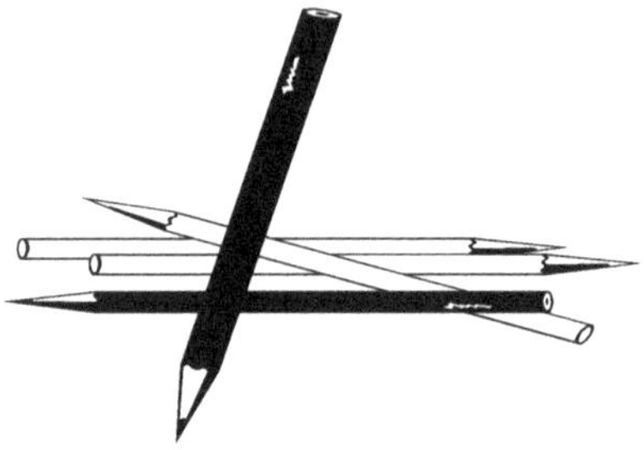

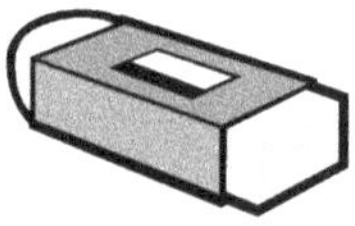

1. ______________ 2. ____________ 3. __________

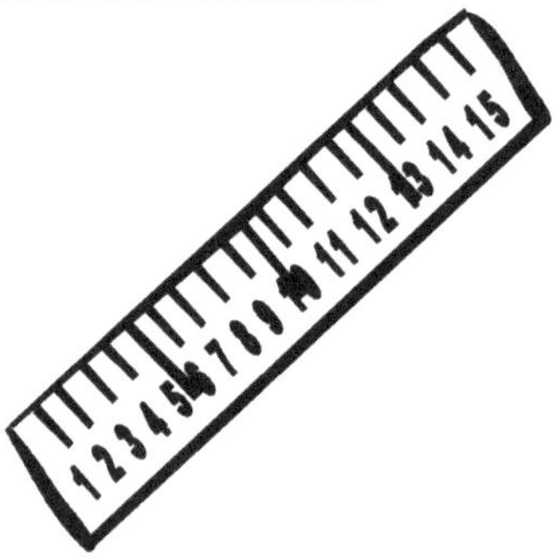

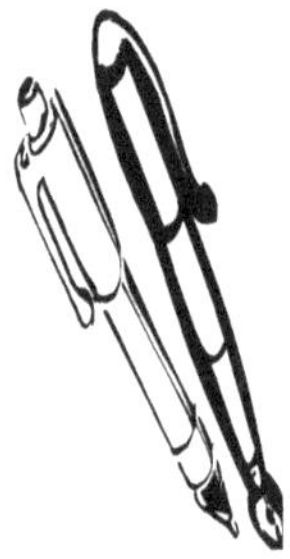

4. __________________

5. ________ 6. ______

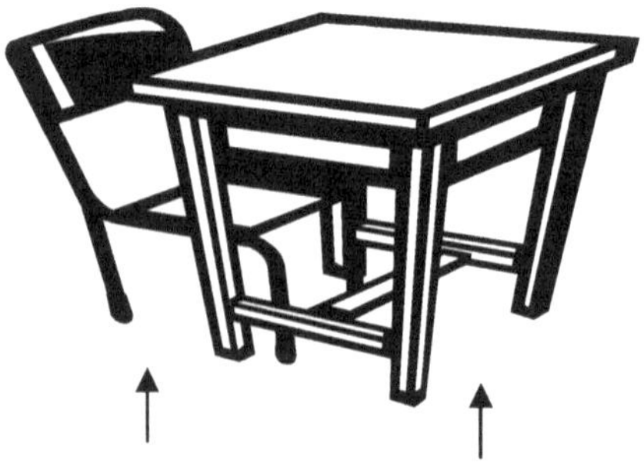

7. ________ and ______ 8. _________

These words are **<u>nouns</u>**.
Nouns are the **names** of **things**.

Things in the classroom

 Write

1.

2.

3.

4.

5.

6.

7.

8.

9.

1.

2.

3. | s |
4. | c |
| i |
5. | s |
| s |
6. | o |
| r |
7. | s |

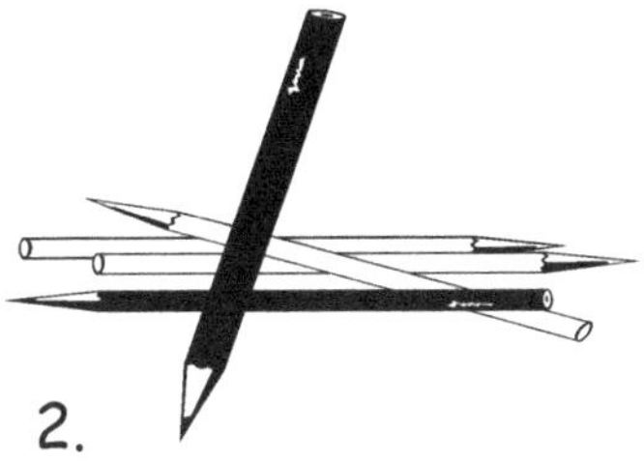

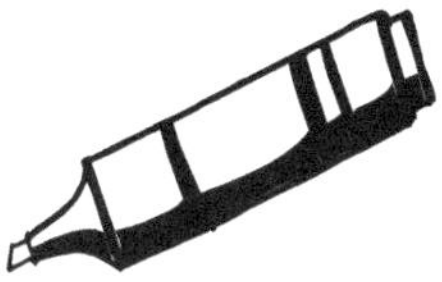

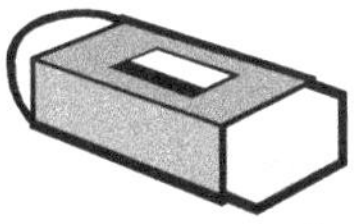

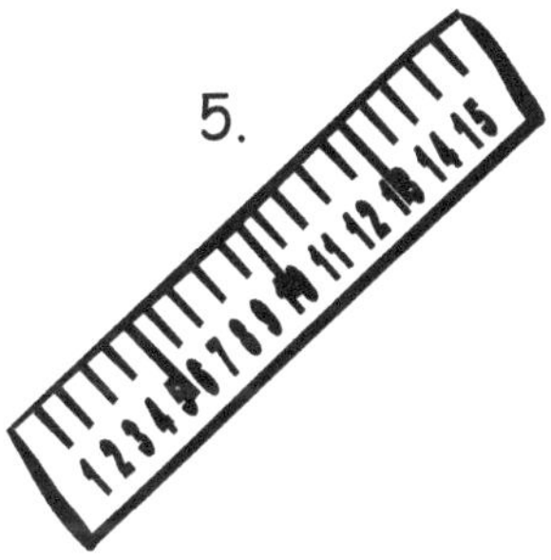

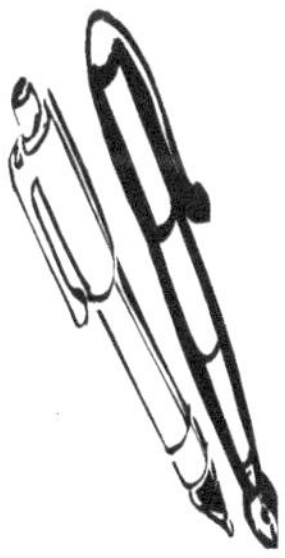

8.

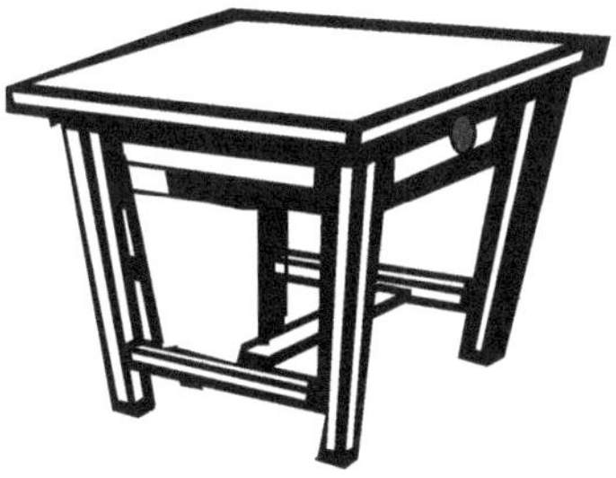

9.

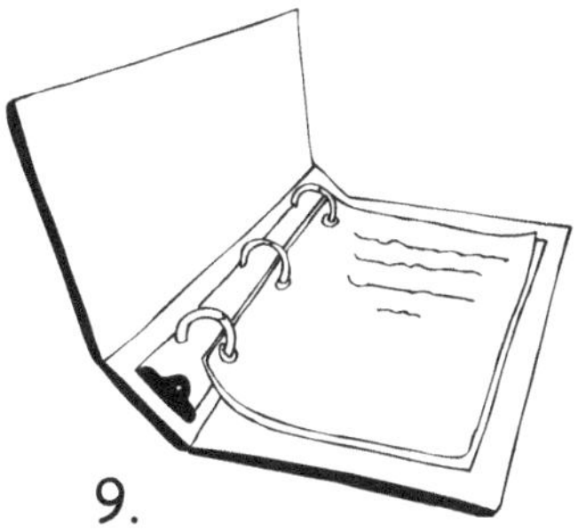

Days of the week 1

Sunday	Monday	Tuesday	Wednesday
Thursday	Friday	Saturday	

Write the days of the week.

1. S __ __ day
2. M __ __ day
3. T __ __ __ day
4. W __ __ __ __ __ day
5. Th __ __ __ day
6. F __ __ day
7. S __ __ __ __ day

Write the days of the week next to the numbers

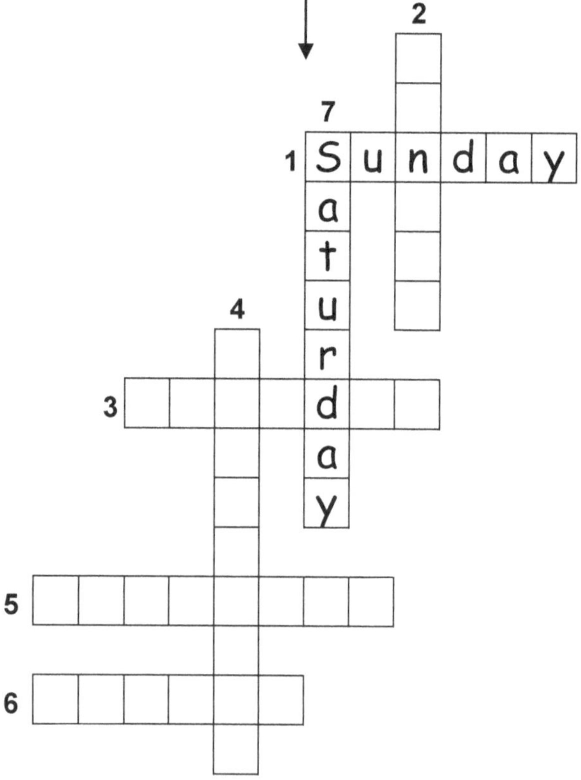

Find and highlight the days of the week.

m	n	S	u	n	d	a	y	s	l	m	z	t	f	q	h	g	d	s	r	t
n	w	s	a	t	y	p	d	M	o	n	d	a	y	p	i	x	c	b	k	j
T	u	e	s	d	a	y	c	b	n	m	q	s	z	t	u	t	m	b	e	r
t	s	c	t	o	W	e	d	n	e	s	d	a	y	k	w	p	s	r	w	y
k	t	h	g	v	x	q	T	h	u	r	s	d	a	y	z	l	g	u	s	t
n	n	F	r	i	d	a	y	s	l	m	z	t	f	q	h	g	d	s	r	t
x	l	z	c	b	r	p	q	e	r	t	S	a	t	u	r	d	a	y	d	b

See months of the year, **page 48**.

Days of the week 2

Today is ______________________________.

Tomorrow is ____________________________.

Yesterday was __________________________.

Time of the day

	1. morning	2. noon
3. afternoon	4. evening	5. night

Write

1. _ _ _ _ _ _ _

2. _ _ _ _

3. _ _ _ _ _ _ _ _ _

4. _ _ _ _ _ _ _

5. _ _ _ _ _

What is the time?

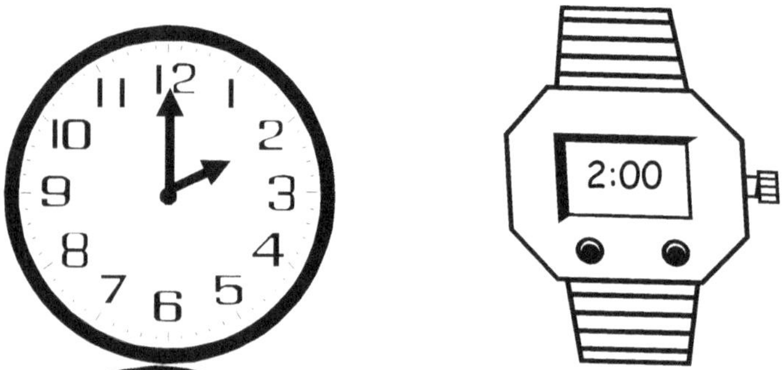

It is two o'clock.

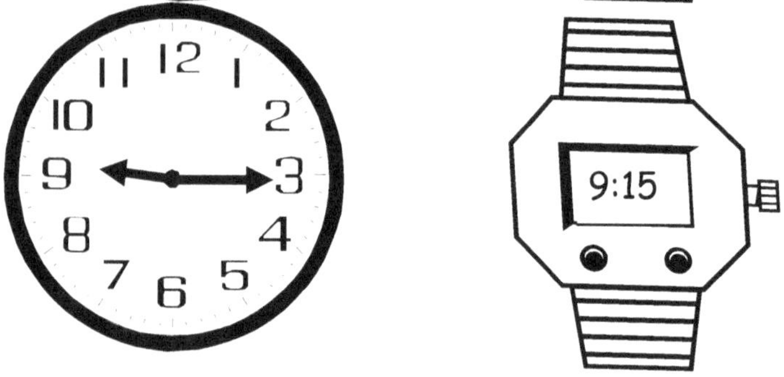

It is nine fifteen.

Write the time with numbers. ↓ Write the time with words. ↓

1

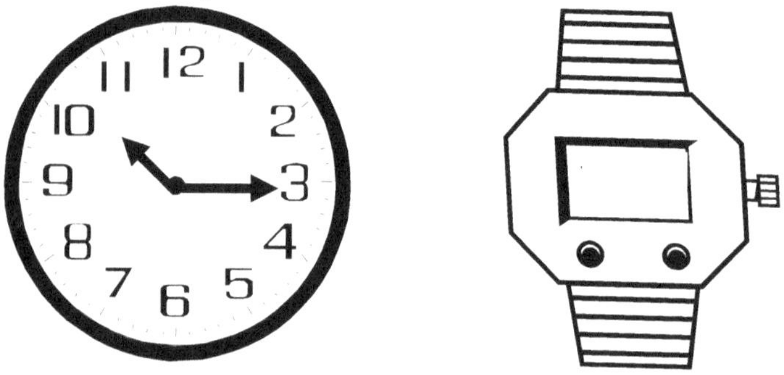

____

2

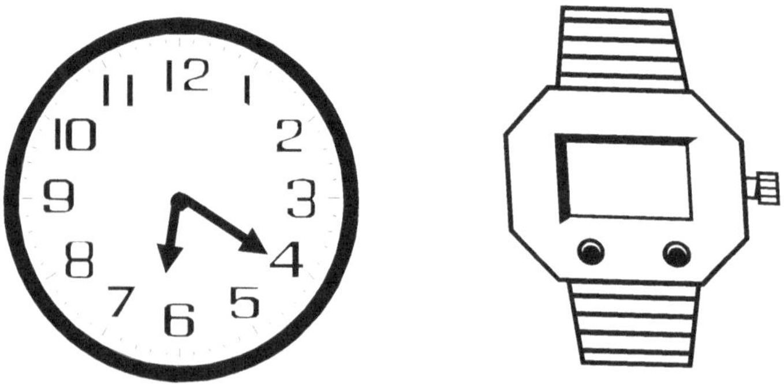

____

3

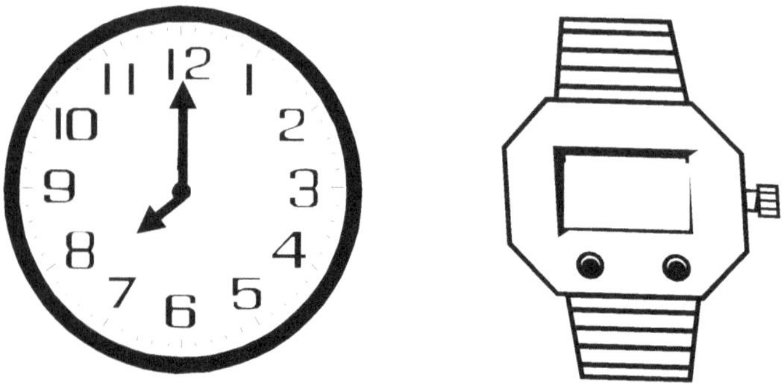

____

What is the time?

Write the time with numbers. Write the time with words.

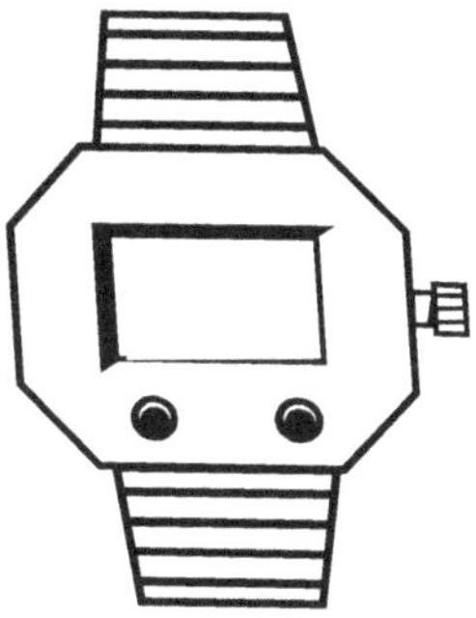

____

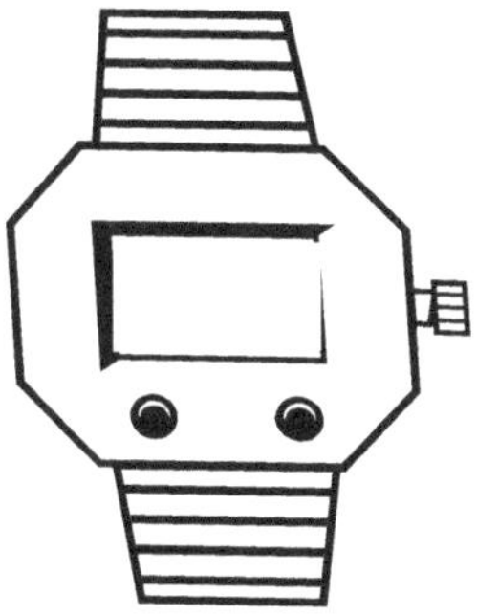

____

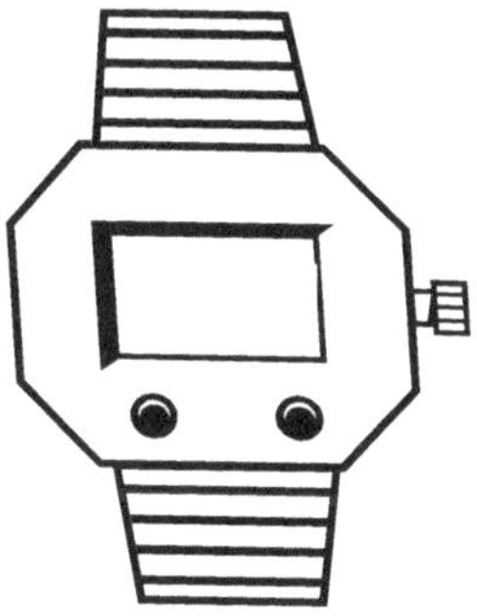

____

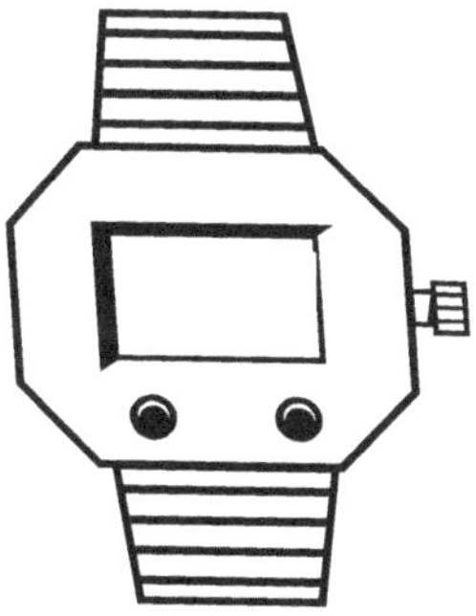

____

What is the time now?

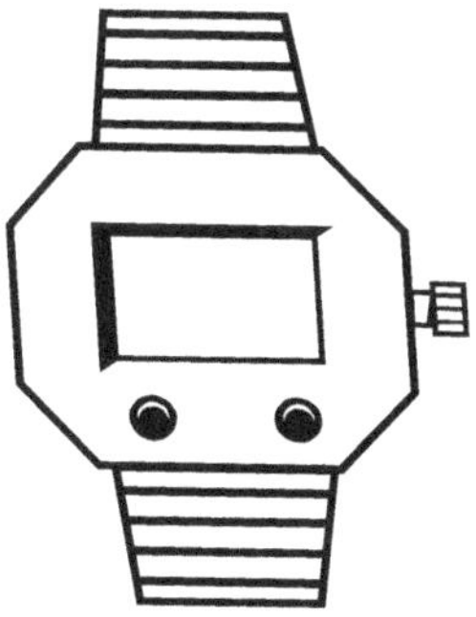

____

Counting things

When we count two or more things we add '**s**' to words. They are plural nouns.

two students  three windows  four books 

 Write

1. *four highlighters*

2. ______ _______

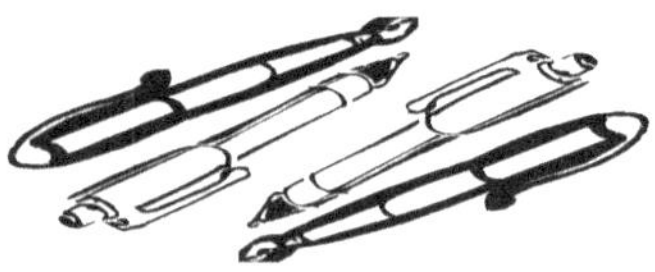 

3. ____ _____

4. ______ ________

5. ___ ________

6. ______ ______

We add '**es**' to some words.

one watch  → two watch<u>**es**</u> 

one box  → two box<u>**es**</u> 

 **Write**

one glass  → two glass __ 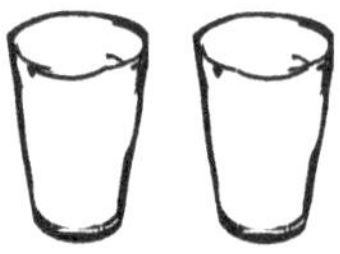

Write the plural nouns.

1. 

2. 

3. 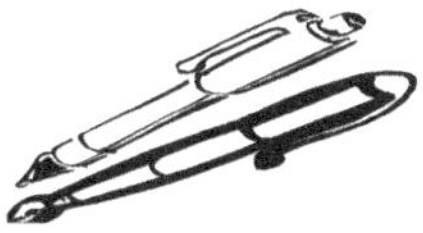

4. 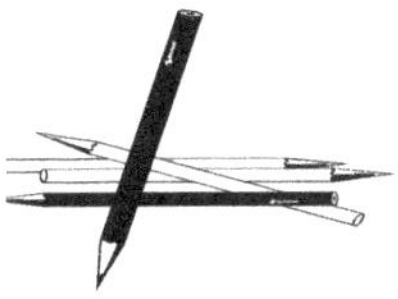

5. 

6. 

7. 

8. 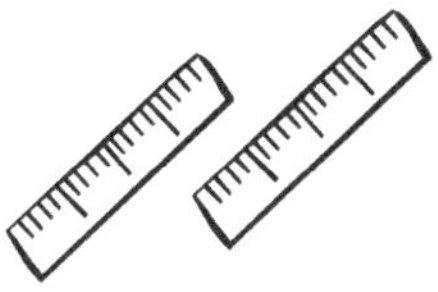

9. 

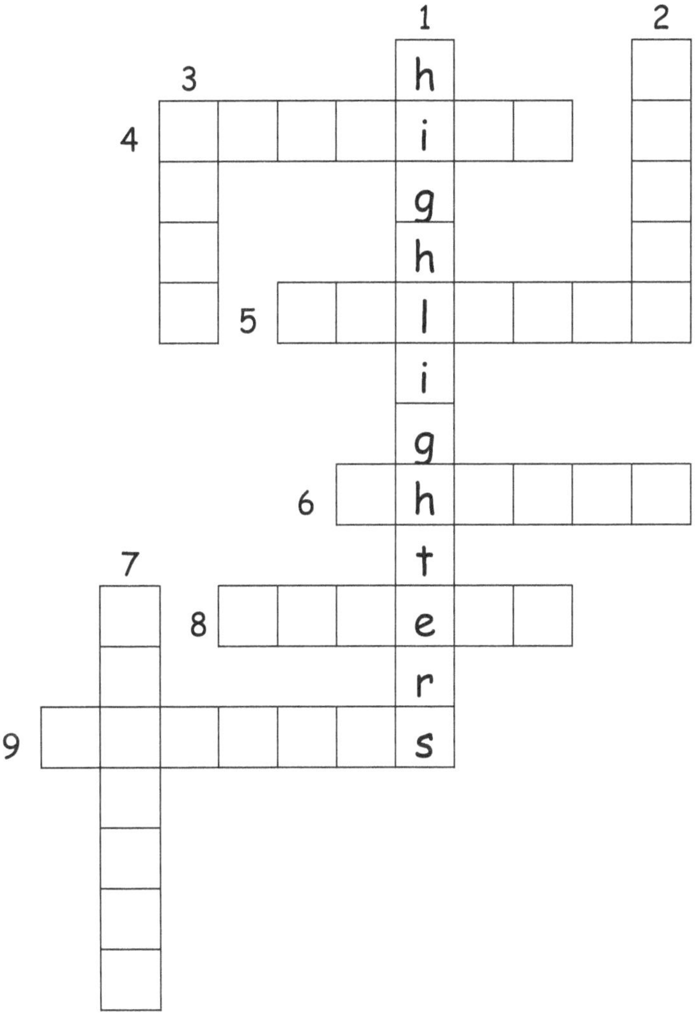

What things can you see in the classroom?

______________________ ______________________

______________________ ______________________

Signs

Read the signs.

1. LIBRARY
2. EXIT
3. CANTEEN
4. NO PARKING
5. ENQUIRIES
6. TOILET

Write the words.

1. _ _ _ _ _ _ _

2. _ _ _ _

3. _ _ _ _ _ _ _

4. _ _ _ _ _ _ _ _ _

5. _ _ _ _ _ _ _ _ _

6. _ _ _ _ _ _

Road signs

1. go left 2. go right 3. do **not** go left 4. do **not** go right

5. do **not** go here 6. No U-Turn - do **not** turn around here

7. walk 8. do **not** walk

Write the words.

1. ______________________________

2. ______________________________

3. ______________________________

4. ______________________________

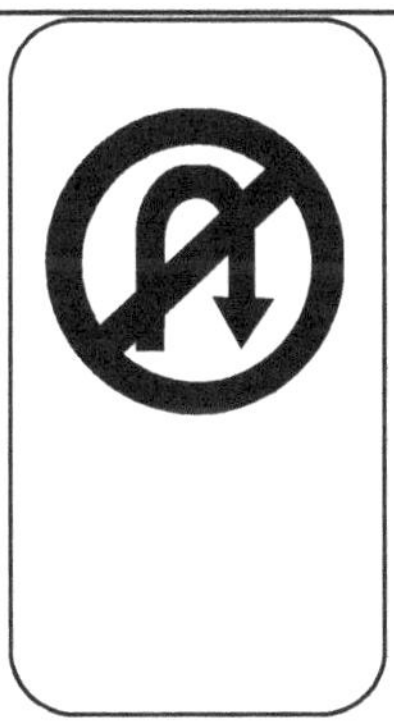

5. ______________________________

6. ______________________________

Put colour here.

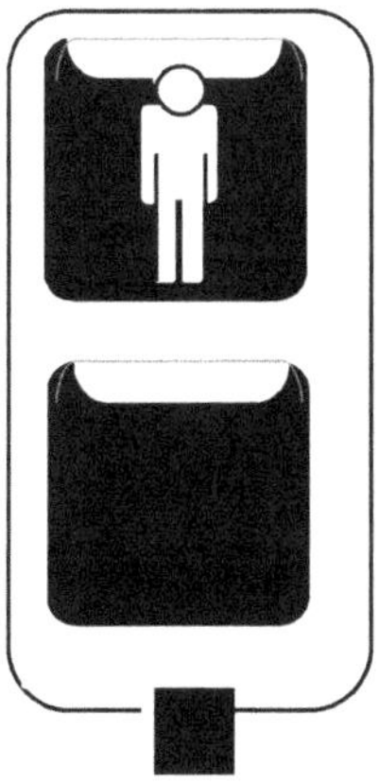

7. ______________________________

8. ______________________________

Signs crossword

Write the words.

1. 

2. 

3 

4. 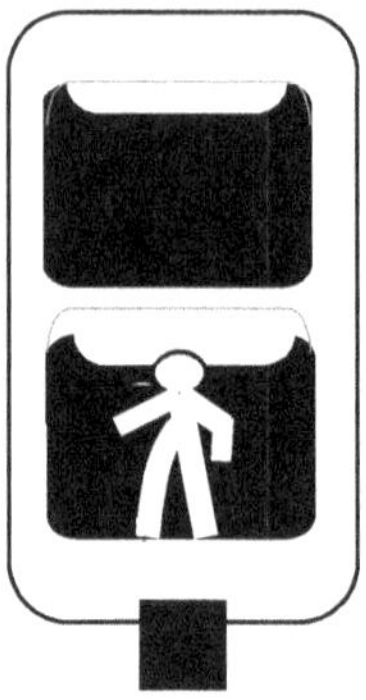

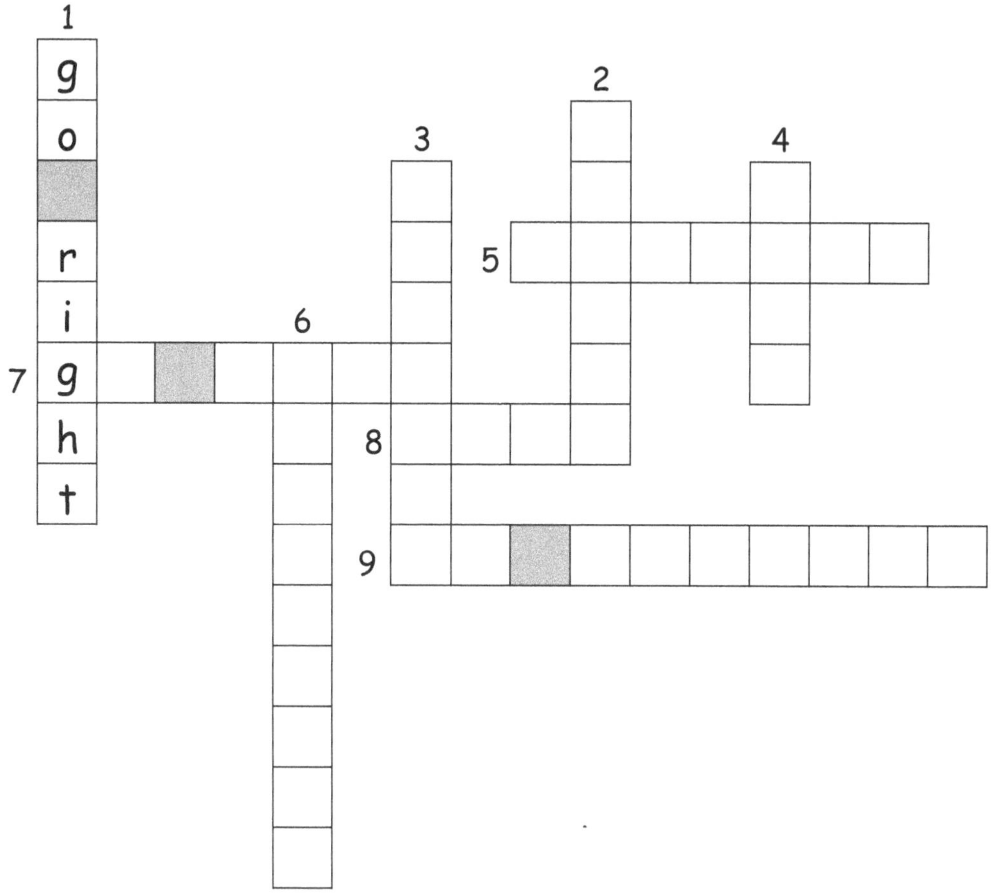

5. 

6. 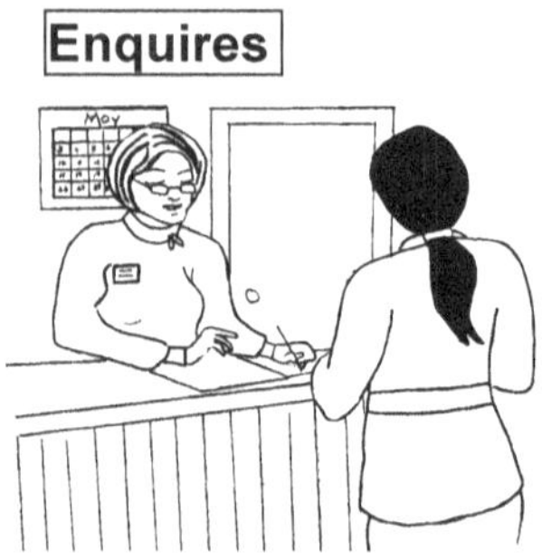

7. 

8. 

9. 

Directions

1. left	2. right	3. straight ahead	4. left	5. right
	6. turn		7. go back	

Write the words.

1. Go _ _ _ _

2. Go _ _ _ _ _

3. Go _ _ _ _ _ _ _ _   _ _ _ _ _

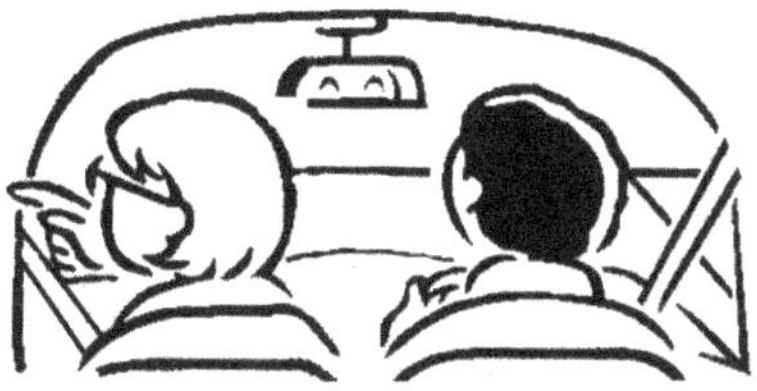

4. Go _ _ _ _

5. Go _ _ _ _ _

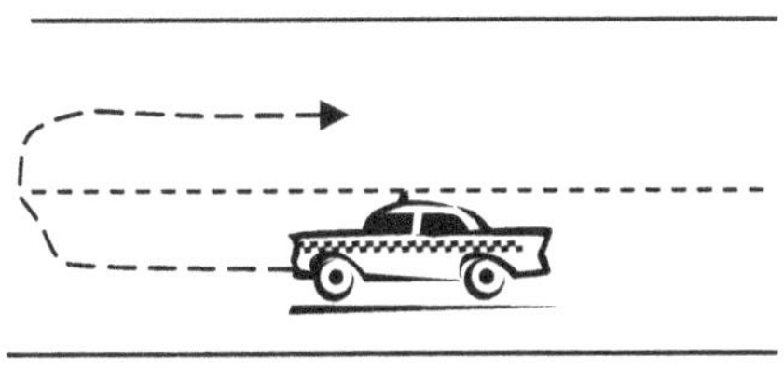

6. _ _ _ _ and go back

7. Turn and _ _ _ _ _ _

People

1. man	2. woman	3. child	4. boy
5. girl	6. men	7. women	
8. children	9. people		

Write 

1. ___ ___ ___

2. ___ ___ ___ ___ ___

3. ___ ___ ___ ___ ___

4. ___ ___ ___

5. ___ ___ ___ ___

6. ___ ___ ___

7. ___ ___ ___ ___ ___

8. ___ ___ ___ ___ ___ ___ ___ ___

9. ___ ___ ___ ___ ___ ___

These words are **nouns.**

<u>**Nouns**</u> are names for **people** and **things.**

People

Write

1. 

2. 

3. 

4. 

5. 

6. 

7. 

8. 

9. 

Family words

1. ~~wife~~	2. mother	3. husband	4. father
5. sister	6. daughter	7. brother	8. son

Write ✍

1. | w | i | f | e | ⟷ 3. ☐☐☐☐☐☐☐

2. ☐☐☐☐☐☐   4. ☐☐☐☐☐☐

5. ☐☐☐☐☐☐ ⟷ 7. ☐☐☐☐☐☐☐

6. ☐☐☐☐☐☐☐☐   8. ☐☐☐

✍ Write the family words

	4			5	
1	w	i	f	e	3 ☐☐☐☐☐☐☐

2 ☐☐☐☐☐☐   8 ☐☐☐☐☐

6 ☐☐☐☐☐☐☐☐

7 ☐☐☐☐☐☐

People, places, things

1. man = he	2. boy = he	3. woman = she	4. girl = she
5. people = they	6. place = it	7. thing = it	

Write: *he, she, they* or *it*

1. __ __

2. __ __

3. __ __ __

4. __ __ __

5. __ __ __ __

6. __ __

7. __ __

Talking about me and other people

1. family	2. son	3. He	4. daughter	5. She
6. mother-in-law	7. father-in-law			
8. They	9. friend	10. She		

Write the words.

This is <u>me</u>.

1. This is my _ _ _ _ _ _ _ .

2. This is my _ _ _.
3. _ _ is eleven years old.

4. This is my _ _ _ _ _ _ _ _ _
5. _ _ _ is twelve years old.

6. This is my _ _ _ _ _ _ _-_ _-_ _ _
7. and _ _ _ _ _ _ _ _ -_ _ -_ _ _.

8. _ _ _ _ _ live near my house.

9. This is my _ _ _ _ _ _ _ .

10. _ _ _ is from South America.

Face

1. forehead	2. hair	3. eyebrow	4. eye	5. ear
6. nose	7. mouth	8. cheek	9. chin	10. neck

Write

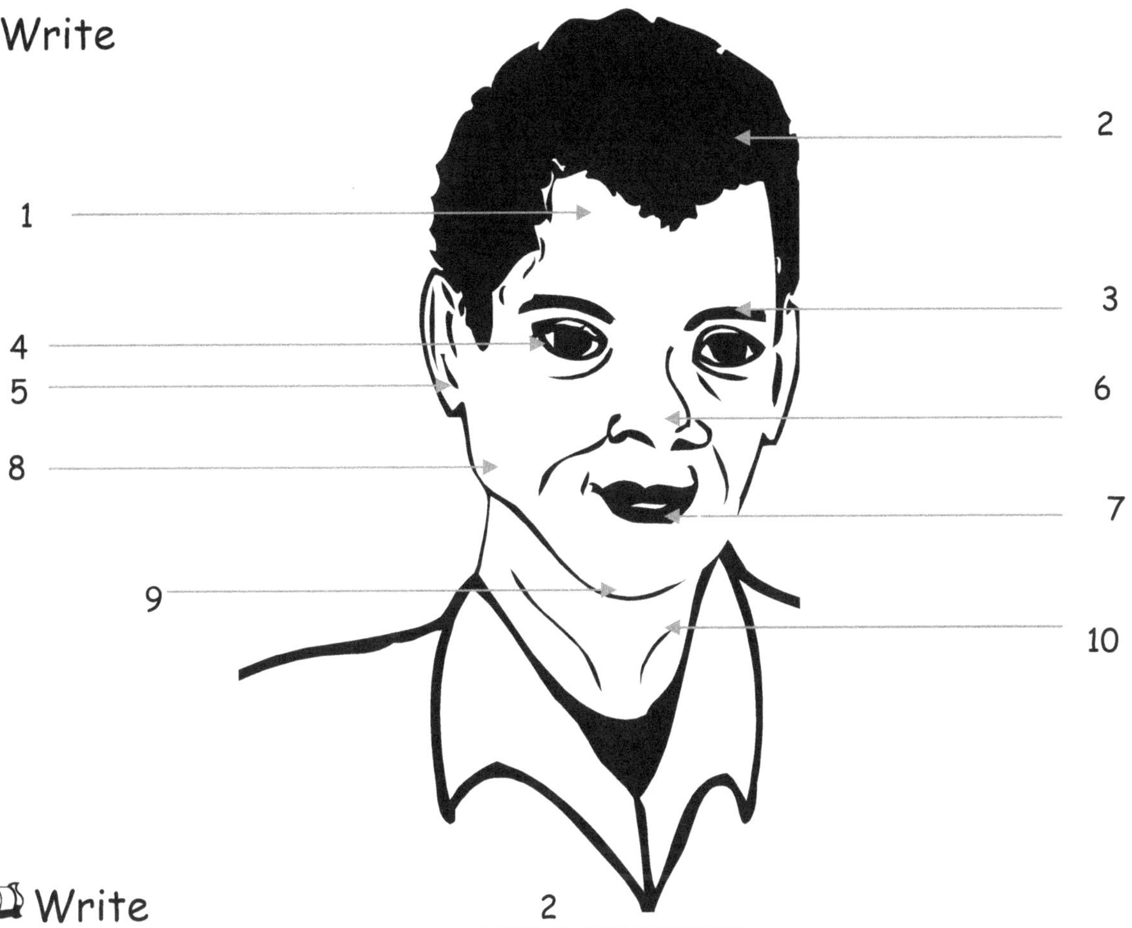

Write

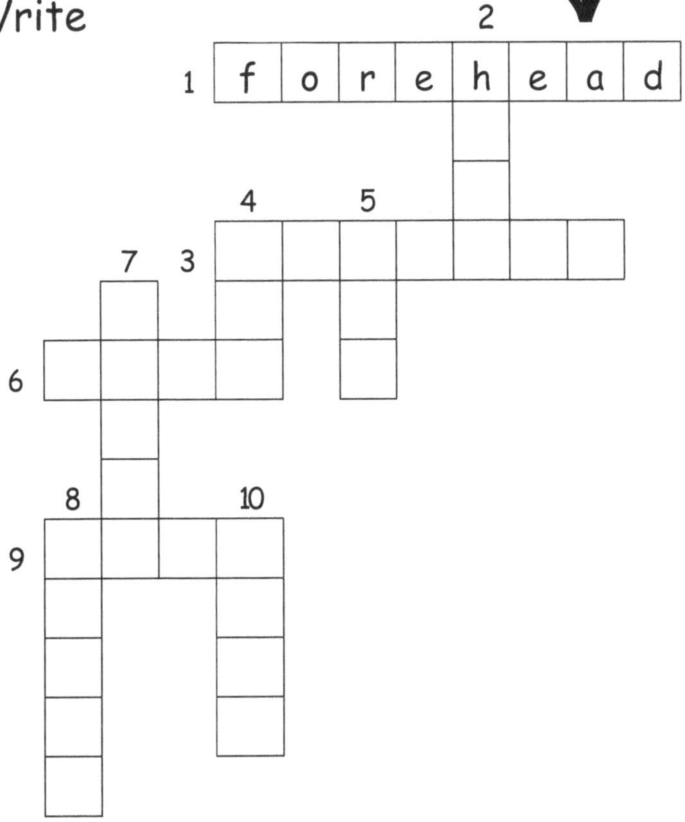

Describing people 1

1. short straight black	2. long straight blonde	3. short curly black
4. bald	5. long wavy blonde	6. short blonde
7. black moustache	8. scarf	9. moustache and a beard
	10. long straight black hair	

1. She has ______________ ______________ hair.

2. She has ______________ ______________ hair.

3. He has ______________ ______________ hair.

4. He is ______________

5. She has ______________ ______________ hair.

6. He has ______________ ______________ hair.

7. He has a ______________ ______________

8. She is wearing a ______________

9. He has a ______________ ______________

10. She has ______________________________ hair.

Write

I have ____

Clothes

1. shirt and tie	2. blouse	3. T-shirt	4. trousers
5. coat	6. skirt	7. suit	8. jeans
9. shorts	10. dress	11. jumper	12. jacket with hood
13. cardigan	14. socks	15. tracksuit	

Write

1.__________and__________ 2.______________ 3.______________ 4.______________

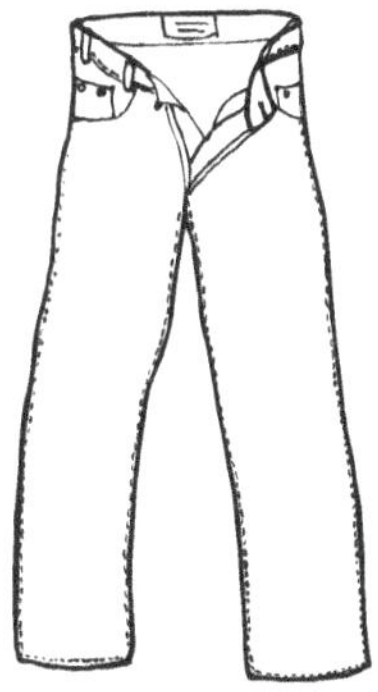

5.______________ 6.______________ 7.______________ 8.______________

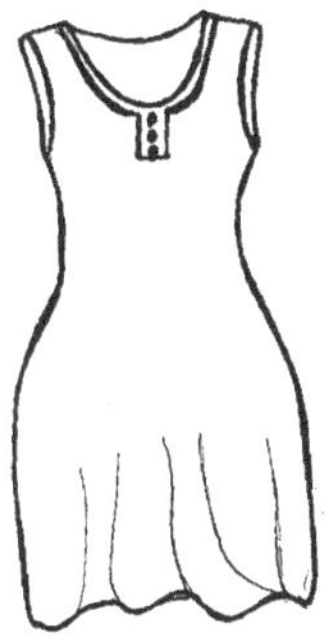

9.______________ 10.______________ 11.______________

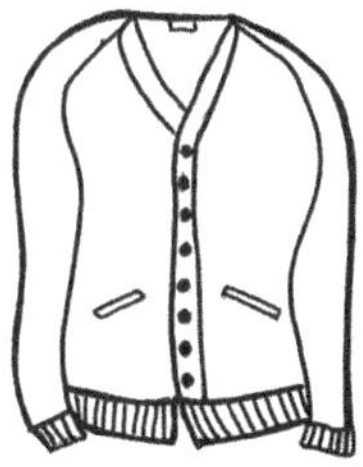

12.__________with__________ 13.______________ 14.______________ 15.______________

Shoes and accessories

1. shoes	2. sandals	3. high heels	4. boots
5. sports shoes	6. belt	7. sunglasses	8. thongs
9. hat	10. cap	11. watch	12. gloves

Write

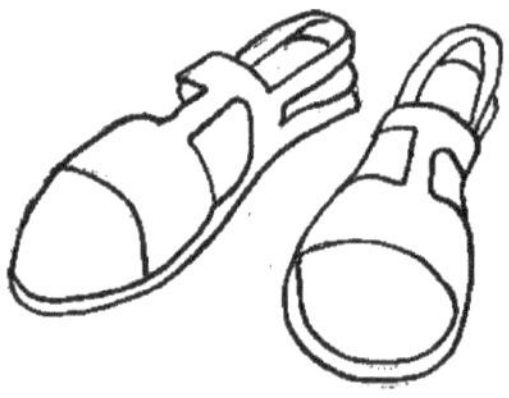

1.______________ 2.______________ 3.______________ 4.______________

5.________ ________ 6.______________ 7.______________ 8.______________

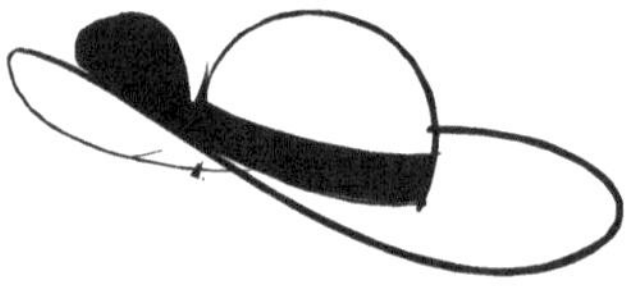

9.______________ 10.______________ 11.______________ 12.______________

What are you wearing?

I am wearing ____

Casual Clothes	Formal Clothes

These words are **nouns**. <u>**Nouns**</u> are names for **people** and **things**.

Clothes and shoes

Write

1. 

2. 

3. 

4. 

5. 

6. 

7. 

8. 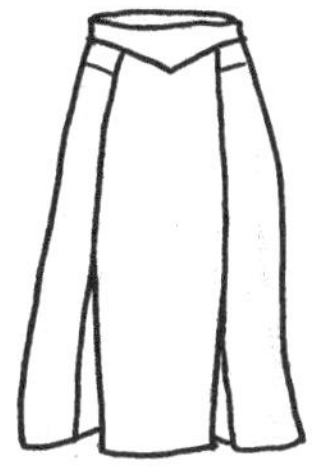

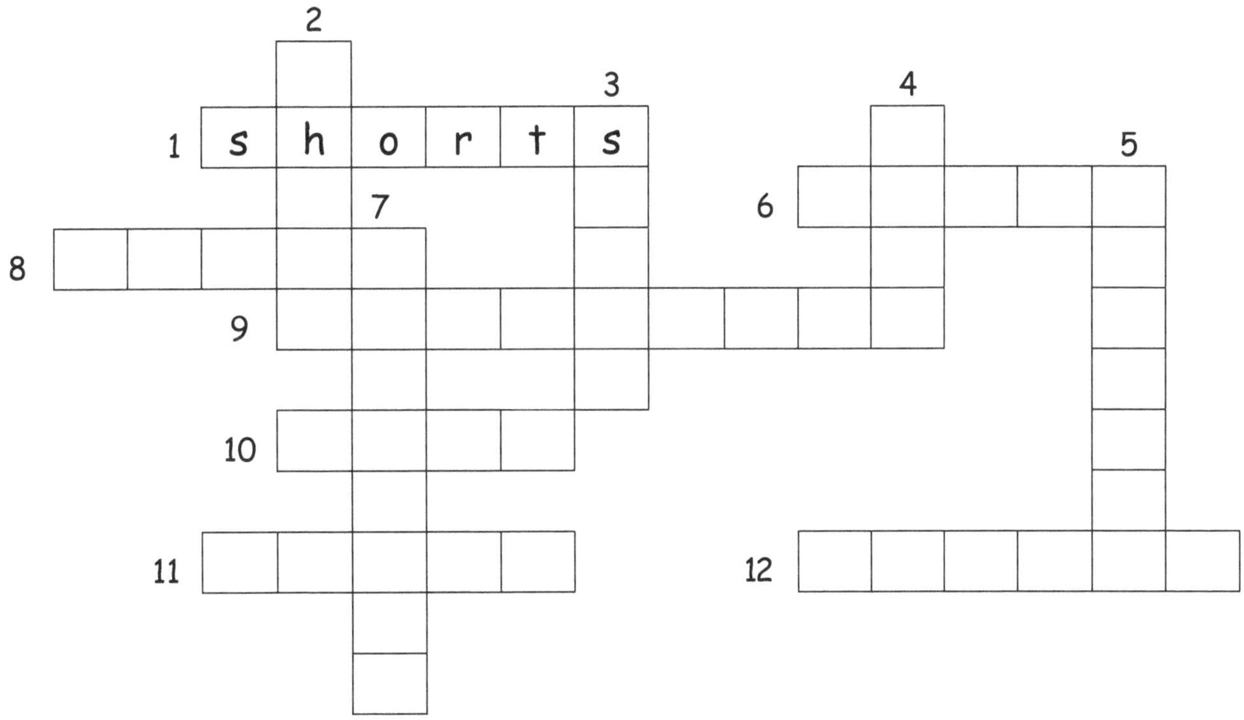

9. 

10. 

11. 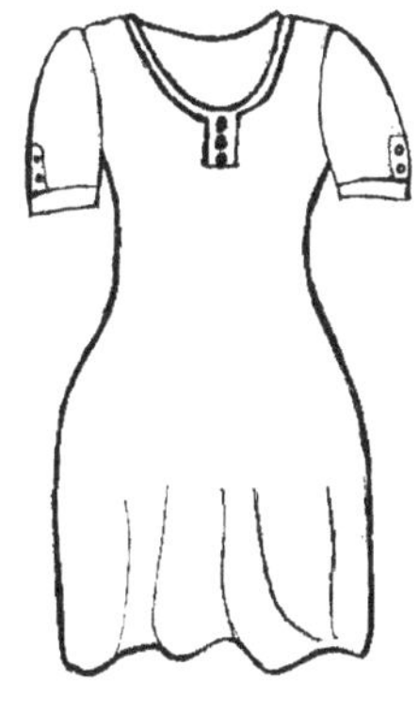

12. 

Describing people 2

1. tracksuits	2. shoes	3. cap	4. T-shirt	5. jeans
6. skirt	7. boots	8. sunglasses		
9. hat	10. shorts	11. sandals		

Write

This is Ray and Pam.
They are wearing
____________[1]
and running ______.[2]

This is Rob.
He is wearing
a ___[3] and
a _-______[4]
and ______.[5]

This is Sally. She is wearing
a blouse and a ______.[6]
She is wearing ______.[7]

This is Con. He is wearing
____________.[8]

This is Lily. She is wearing
a ___[9] and a T-shirt and
______[10] and ________.[11]

Describing people 3

1. tall	2. thin	3. young	4. bald	5. overweight
	6. short		7. middle-aged	

Write

This is Jong. He is _____[1], _____[2] and _____[3].

This is Lee. He is _____[4] and he is ____________[5].

This is Wei. She is ______[6].

Lee and Wei are _______-_____[7].

Write: Jong is wearing a ____________________

Lee is wearing a ____________________

Wei is wearing a ____________________

Everyday activities

1. walk	2. cook	3. watch	4. write	5. drive
6. sing	7. listen	8. drink	9. read	10. shop

Write

1. __ __ __ __

2. __ __ __ __

3. __ __ __ __ __ TV

4. __ __ __ __ __

5. __ __ __ __ __

6. __ __ __ __

7. __ __ __ __ __ __

8. __ __ __ __ __ tea

9. __ __ __ __

10. __ __ __ __

These words are **verbs**.
Verbs say what we **do**.

Write: I ____________________ everyday.

What can you do?

1. draw	2. ride a bicycle	3. play the guitar
4. sew	5. use a computer	6. play cards
7. swim	8. dance	9. make cakes

Write

1. _ _ _ _ _   2. _ _ _ _ _ _ _ _ _ _ _ _ _   3. _ _ _ _ _ _ _ _ _ _ _ _ _

4. _ _ _   5. _ _ _ _ _ _ _ _ _ _ _ _   6. _ _ _ _ _ _ _ _ _

7. _ _ _ _   8. _ _ _ _ _   9. _ _ _ _ _ _ _ _ _

I **can** drive. ✓ 

I **can't** cook. 

I **can** dance. ✓ 

I **can't** swim. 

can't = can not **X**

Write: I can ______________________________

I can't ______________________________

Everyday activities

Write the verbs.

1. 
2. 
3. 
4. 
5. 
6. 
7. 
8. 

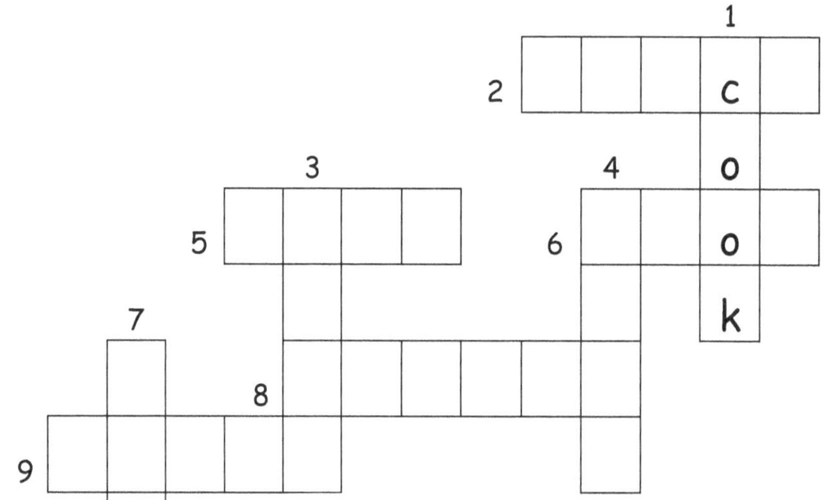

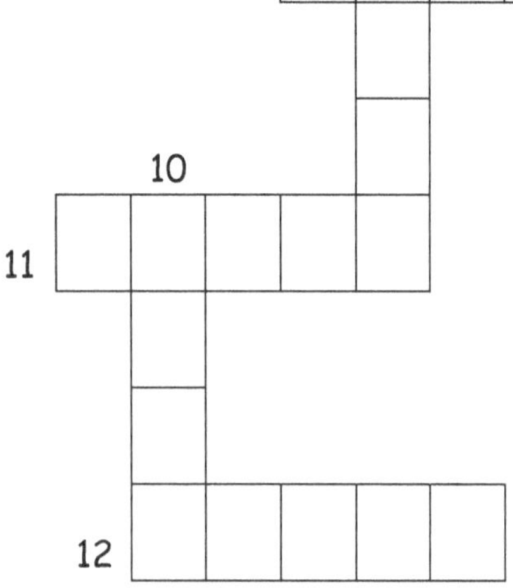

9. 
10. 
11. 
12. 

What do you like doing?

1. fishing	2. cycling	3. running	4. sewing
5. swimming	6. playing games	7. flying	
8. dancing	9. watching sport	10. drawing	

Write

1. _ _ _ _ _ _ _ _

2. _ _ _ _ _ _ _ _

3. _ _ _ _ _ _ _ _

4. _ _ _ _ _ _ _

5. _ _ _ _ _ _ _ _ _ _

6. _ _ _ _ _ _ _ _ _ _ _ _ _ _ _

7. _ _ _ _ _ _ _

8. _ _ _ _ _ _ _ _

9. _ _ _ _ _ _ _ _ _ _ _ _ _ _ _ _

10. _ _ _ _ _ _ _ _

Write

☺ I like ________________________________.

☹ I don't like ____________________________.

Sport

1. volley ball	2. golf	3. soccer	4. baseball
5. cricket	6. hockey	7. tennis	8. table tennis

Write

1. _________ 2. ________ 3. ________

4. _________ 5. ________ 6. ________

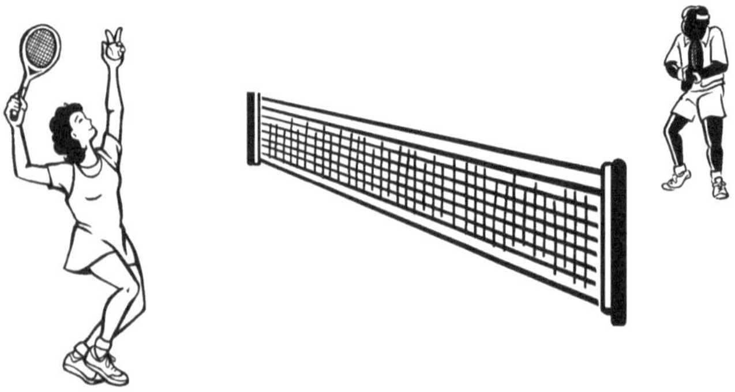

7. _______ 8. ______ ______

Write I like playing ____________________ ☺

I like watching____________________ ☺

Sport

Write

1. 

2. 

3. 

4. 

5. 

6. 

7. 

8. 

Jobs

1. builder	2. mechanic	3. chef	4. plumber	5. teacher
6. cleaner	7. electrician	8. hairdresser	9. shop assistant	

Write

1. ____________ 2. ____________ 3. ____________

4. ____________ 5. ____________ 6. ____________

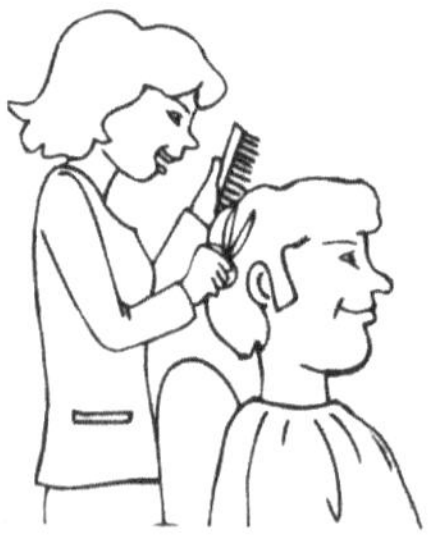

7. ____________ 8. ____________ 9. ____________

Jobs

10. policeman	11. doctor	12. nurse
13. painter	14. librarian	15. dentist

10. ____________________

11. ____________________

12. ____________________

13. ____________________

14. ____________________

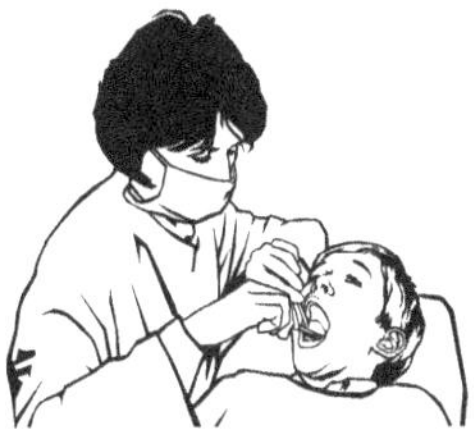

15. ____________________

Write

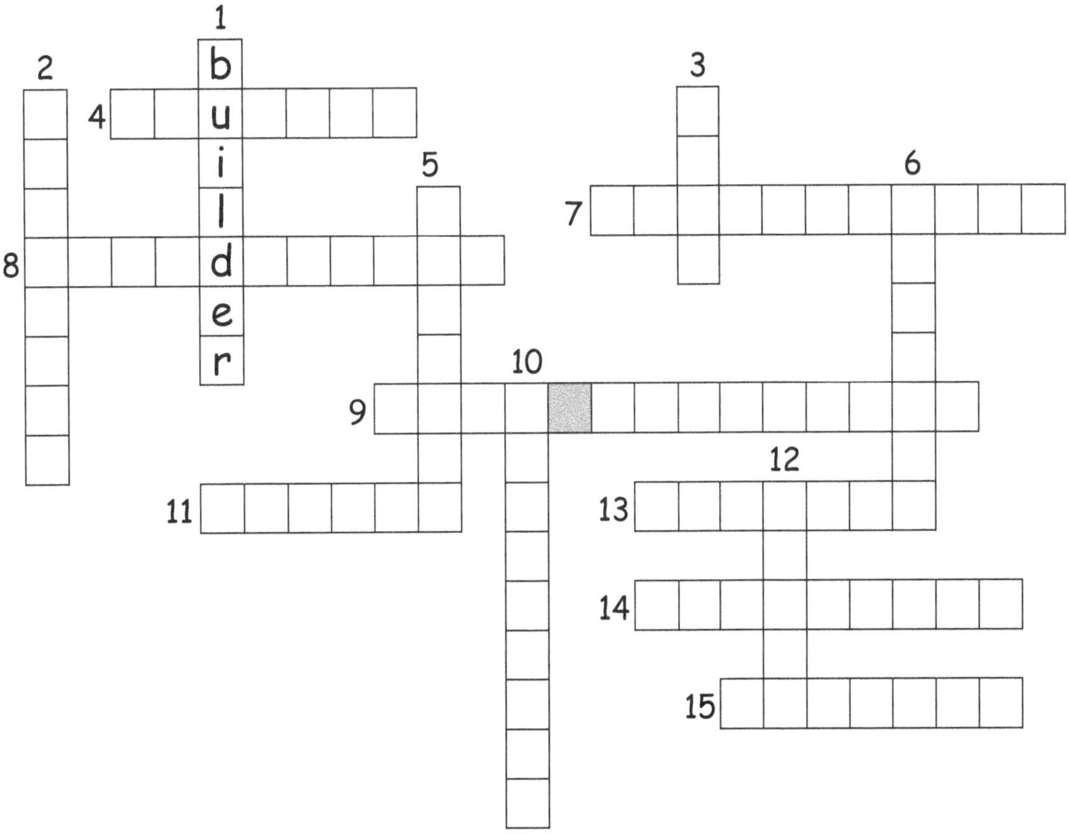

Months

1. January	2. February	3. March	4. April
5. May	6. June	7. July	8. August
9. September	10. October	11. November	12. December

Write the twelve months of the year.

1. J __ __ __ __ __ y
2. F __ __ __ __ __ __ y
3. M __ __ ch
4. A __ __ __ __
5. M __ __
6. J __ __ e
7. J __ __ y
8. A __ __ __ __ t
9. S __ __ __ __ __ __ er
10. O __ __ __ __ er
11. N __ __ __ __ __ er
12. D __ __ __ __ __ er

Highlight the twelve months of the year.

The names of months begin with a capital letter.

w	s	M	a	y	g	l	z	u	p	l	k	M	a	r	c	h	t	p	z	x
n	w	a	a	t	y	p	d	F	e	b	r	u	a	r	y	x	c	b	k	j
d	f	n	r	k	l	z	c	b	n	m	q	S	e	p	t	e	m	b	e	r
t	O	c	t	o	b	e	r	x	J	u	n	e	k	y	w	p	s	r	w	y
k	t	h	g	v	x	q	y	f	u	r	b	z	y	r	A	u	g	u	s	t
n	n	j	z	x	m	q	l	s	l	m	z	t	f	q	h	g	d	s	r	t
x	l	z	J	a	n	u	a	r	y	x	D	e	c	e	m	b	e	r	q	b
N	o	v	e	m	b	e	r	h	q	r	t	A	p	r	i	l	h	j	k	n

Calendar

Write

This year is 2 _ _ _

This month is ____________

Write numbers for dates for this month on the calendar.

The date today is:

____

Seasons of the year

Write the three months for each season where you live.

Summer 	**Autumn** 
Winter 	**Spring** 

The season now is ____________________

Jack's daily routine

1. wake up	2. get up	3. have breakfast	4. have a shower
5. go to work	6. watch television	7. have dinner	8. go to sleep

Write

1. _ _ _ _   _ _

2. _ _ _   _ _

3. _ _ _ _   _ _ _ _ _ _ _ _ _

4. _ _ _ _   _   _ _ _ _ _ _

6. _ _ _ _ _   _ _ _ _ _ _ _ _ _ _

5. _ _   _ _   _ _ _ _

7. _ _ _ _   _ _ _ _ _ _

8. _ _   _ _   _ _ _ _ _

Daily routine

Write the words next to the numbers.

What time?

Write answers about Jack. Write answers about you.

1. What time does Jack get up? ____________ ____________
2. What time does he have breakfast? ____________ ____________
3. What time does he watch television? ____________ ____________
4. What time does he have dinner? ____________ ____________
5. What time does he go to sleep? ____________ ____________

Special days

	1. Christmas	2. New Year	3. birthday
4. Easter	5. engagement	6. wedding	7. funeral

Write

1. _ _ _ _ _ _ _ _ _ _
2. _ _ _ _ _ _ _
3. _ _ _ _ _ _ _ _ _

4. _ _ _ _ _ _
5. _ _ _ _ _ _ _ _ _ _ _ _
6. _ _ _ _ _ _ _ _

7. _ _ _ _ _ _ _

Special cards for special days

Write

Merry Christmas

Happy New Year!

1. 

2. ___ ____

Happy
Birthday

Happy
Easter!

3. _________

4. ______

Congratulations
on your Engagement

5. ___________

Best wishes
on your
special day

6. _______

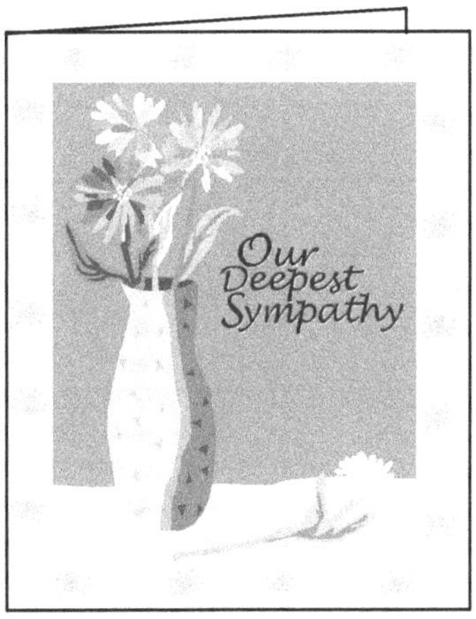
Our
Deepest
Sympathy

7. _______

Past, present and future time

Write the words

now	yesterday	did	tomorrow	last month
next month	at present	last year	next year	will

past time	present time	future time

Write

past time	present time	future time
Last year **20_ _**	**This year** **20_ _**	**Next year** **20_ _**

Write the month.

past time	present time	future time
Last month was ________________	This month is ________________	Next month will be ________________

Write the day.

past time	present time	future time
Yesterday was ________________	Today is ________________	Tomorrow will be ________________

We use **verbs** to show past, present and future time.

Past time

We write '**ed**' on the end of some verbs to talk about the past.

Highlight the past verbs

1. Yesterday I walked in the park with my friend.

2. Yesterday I cooked food for my friends.

3. Last night I watched a movie on TV with my family.

4. Last night I listened to music.

5. Yesterday I shopped for food and other things.

6. Last week I played cards with my friends.

Write the highlighted verbs in the crossword.

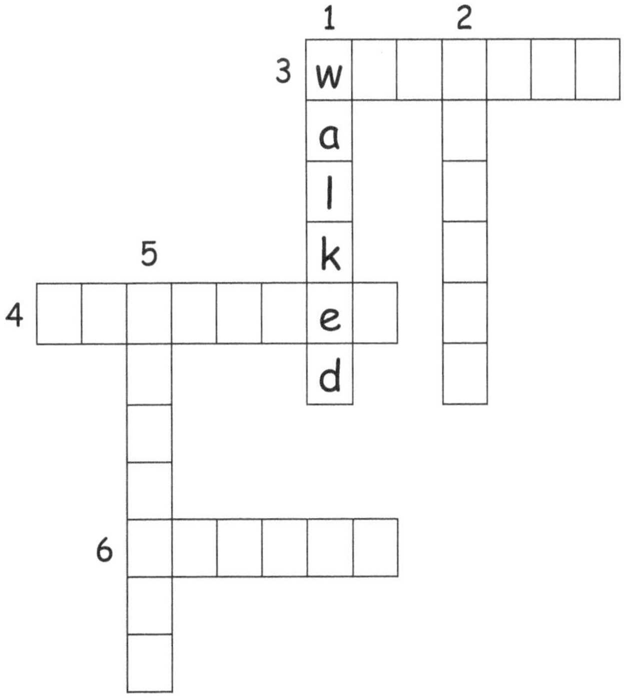

Write: Yesterday I ______________________________

More past tense verbs

We change the spelling of some verbs when we talk about the past.

present		past
is	→	was
go	→	went
do	→	did
see	→	saw
buy	→	bought
come	→	came

Highlight the past verbs.

1. Yesterday was hot.
2. I went to the supermarket yesterday.
3. I did my homework last night.
4. I saw a kangaroo last week.
5. Yesterday I bought new shoes.
6. We came to this country last year.

Write a past verb in each sentence.

1. Yesterday _________ hot.

2. I ___________ to the supermarket yesterday.

3. I _________ my homework last night.

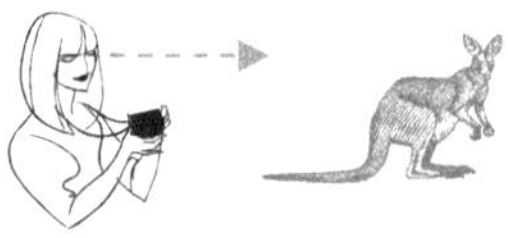

4. I _________ a kangaroo last week.

5. Yesterday I _________ new shoes.

6. We ________ to this country last year.

Past and future

Write the day. Write the day.

Yesterday was__________. Tomorrow will be___________.

Highlight verbs in the **past** and **future** sentences.

Yesterday I walked in the park.  Tomorrow I will walk in the park.

Yesterday I cooked chicken.  Tomorrow I will cook chicken.

Yesterday I watched TV.  Tomorrow I will watch TV.

Yesterday I listened to music.  Tomorrow I will listen to music.

Yesterday I shopped for food.  Tomorrow I will shop for food.

Yesterday I talked to my friend.  Tomorrow I will talk to my friend.

Yesterday I played cards.  Tomorrow I will play cards.

Write

Yesterday I ____________________ Tomorrow I ____________________

Yesterday I ____________________ Tomorrow I ____________________

Health – Parts of the Body

1. ~~head~~	2. hair	3. neck	4. shoulders
5. chest	6. back	7. stomach	8. arms
9. hands	10. fingers	11. legs	12. feet

Write

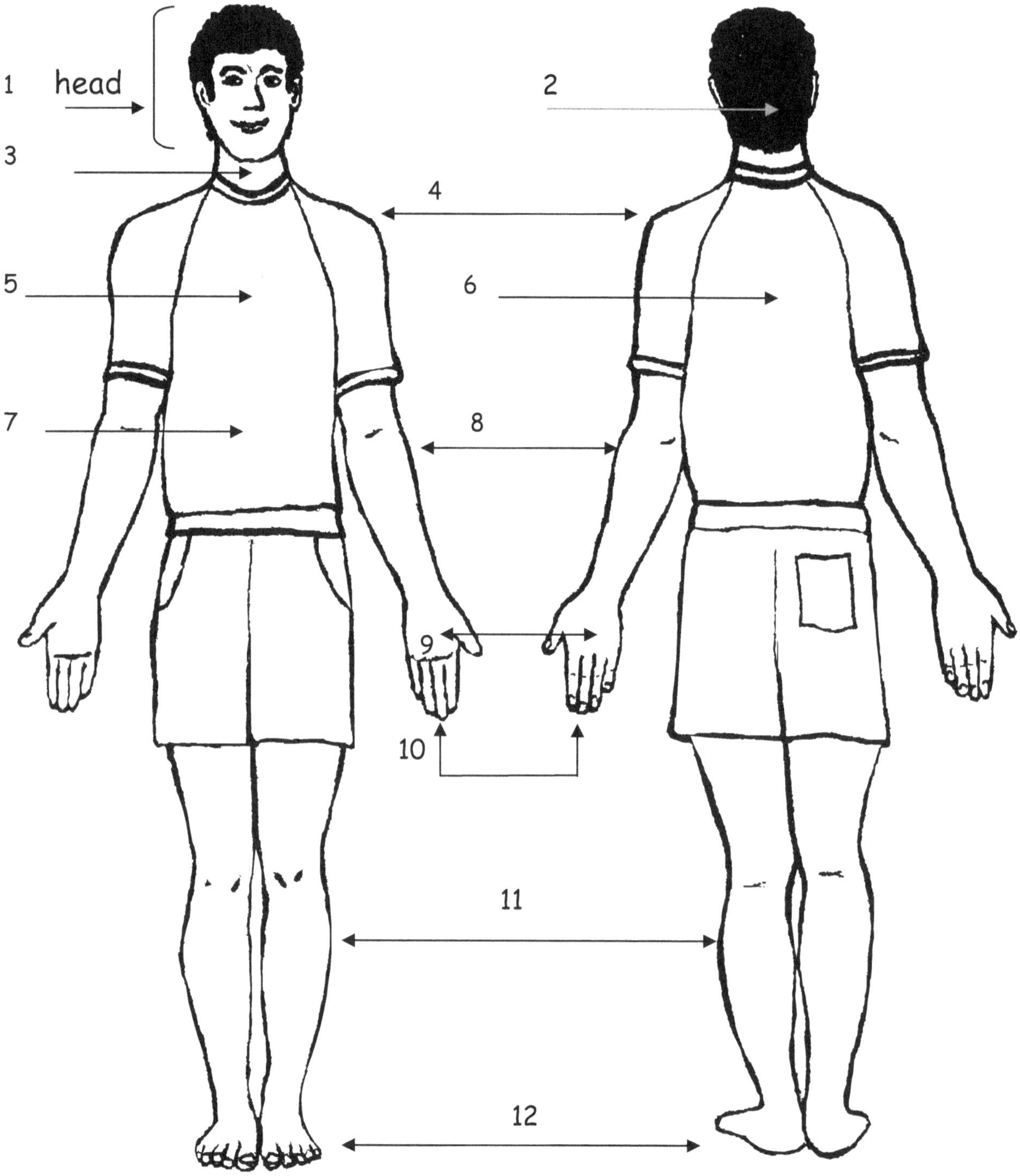

Parts of the Body

Write the words next to the numbers.

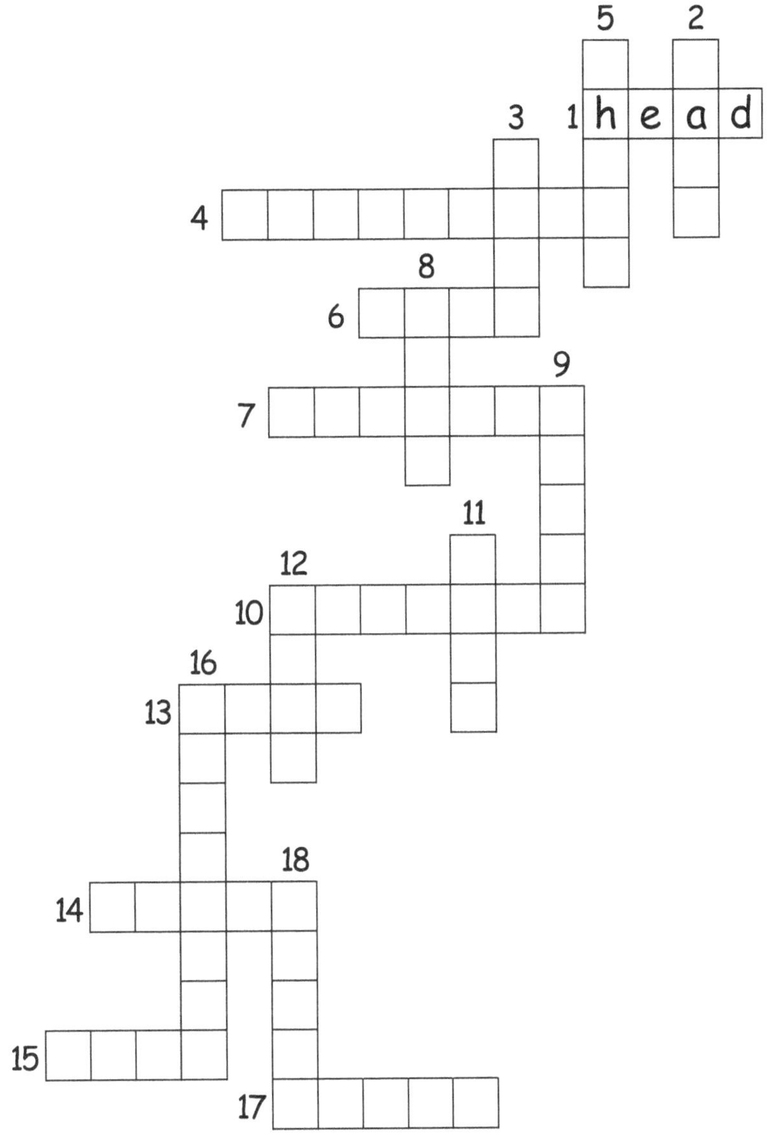

13. knee 14. ankle 15. toes 16. knuckles 17. wrist 18. elbow

Write

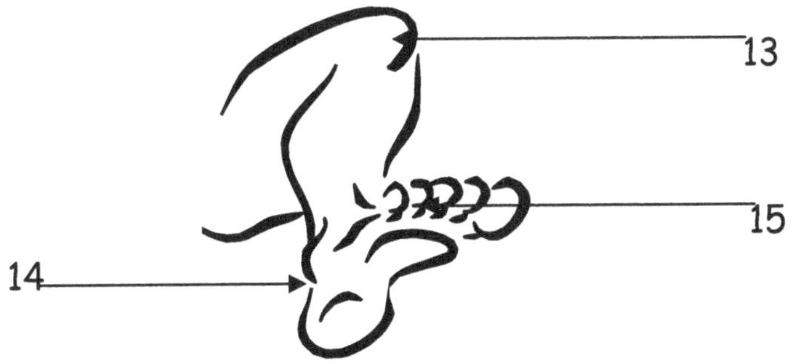

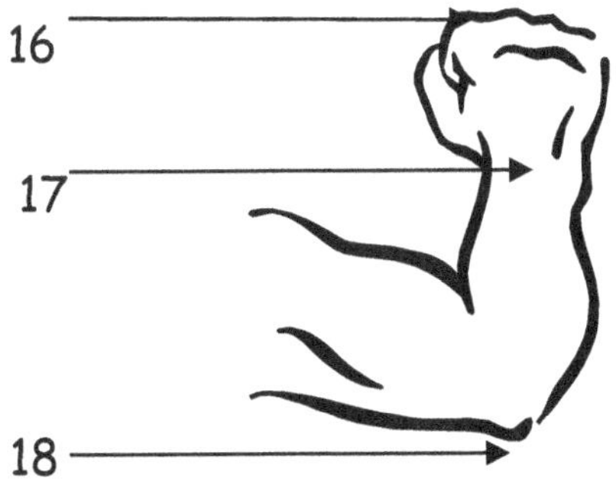

Symptoms

1. a headache	2. back pain	3. a rash	4. asthma
5. a fever	6. a sore throat	7. a stomach ache	
8. a runny nose	9. sore eye		

Write

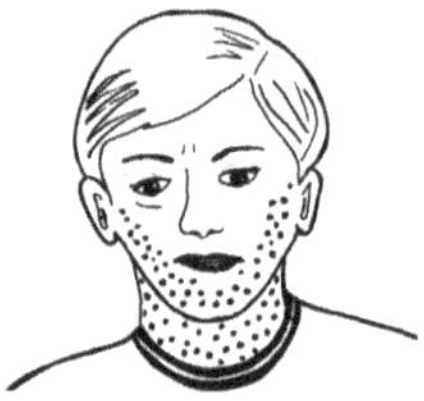

1. ________________ 2. ________________ 3. ________________

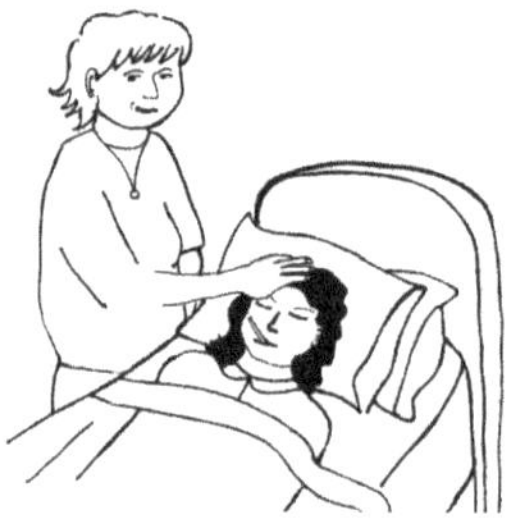

4. ________________ 5. ________________ 6. ________________

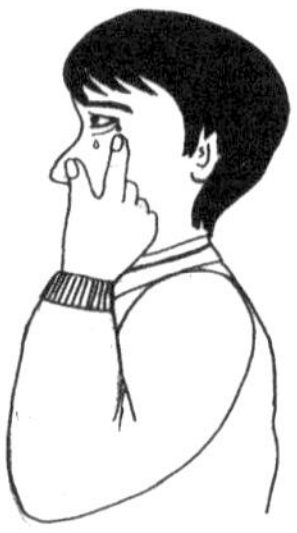

7. ________________ 8. ________________ 9. ________________

We can **ask:** What is the matter?

We can **say:** He has ______________________________

She has______________________________

I have ______________________________

What is the matter?

Write

1. She has a _ _ _ _ _ _ _ _ _

2. He has _ _ _ _ _ _ _ _

3. He has a _ _ _ _

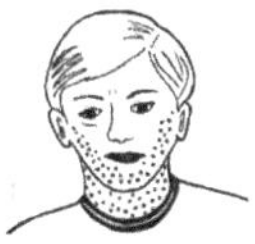

4. She has a _ _ _ _ _

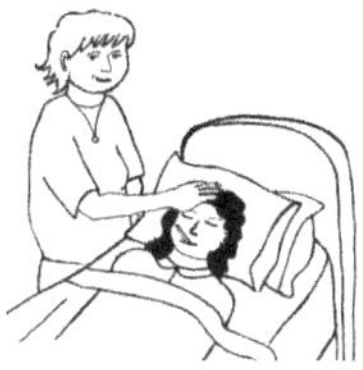

5. He has a _ _ _ _ _ _ _ _ _ _ _ _

6. He has a _ _ _ _ _ _ _ _ _ _

7. She has _ _ _ _ _ _

8. He has a _ _ _ _ _ _ _

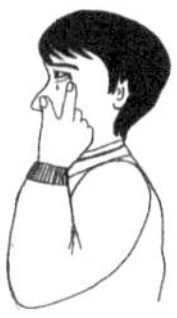

9. He has a _ _ _ _ _ _ _ _ _

Write

Medical check-up

1. x-ray	2. blood pressure check	3. blood test
4. breathing test	5. throat examination	6. temperature check
7. ECG	8. body scan (MRI)	9. ultrasound

Write

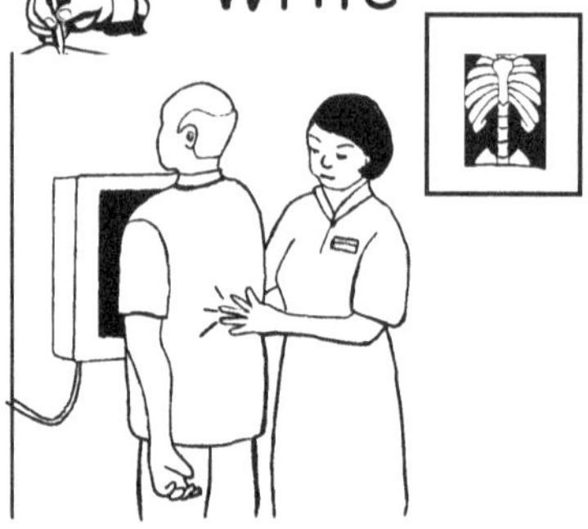

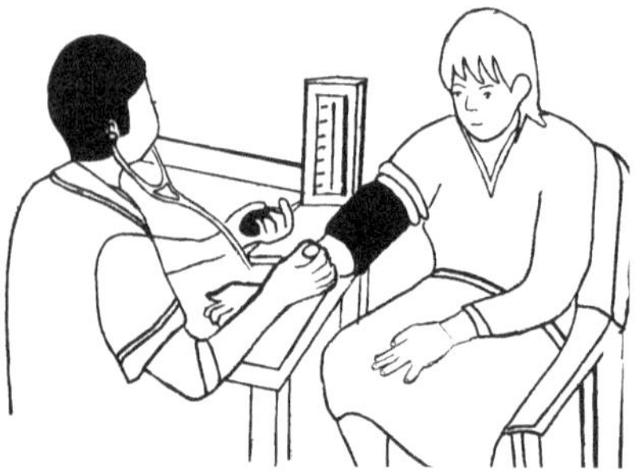

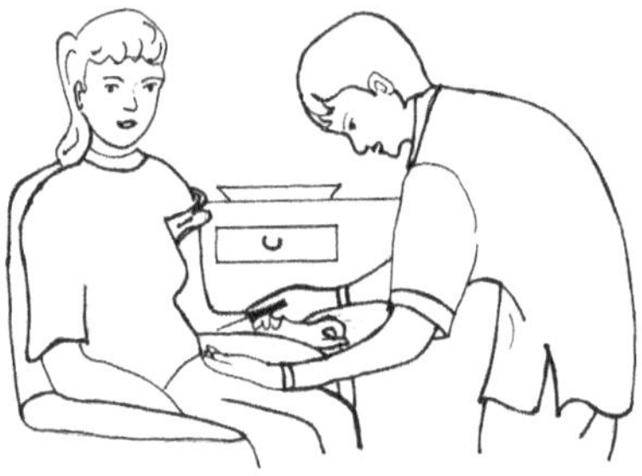

1. _ - _ _ _

2. _

3. _ _ _ _ _ _ _ _ _ _

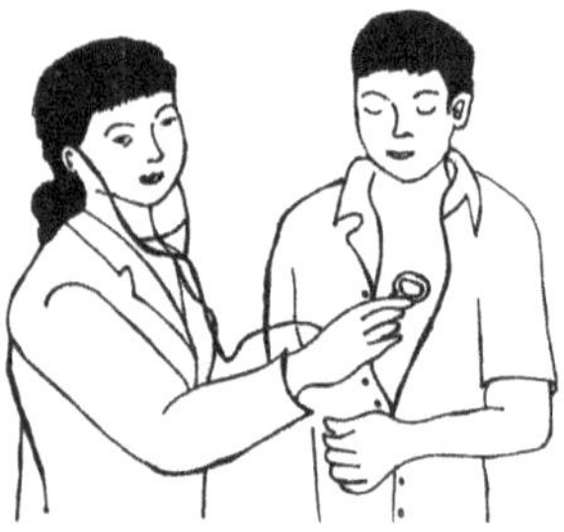

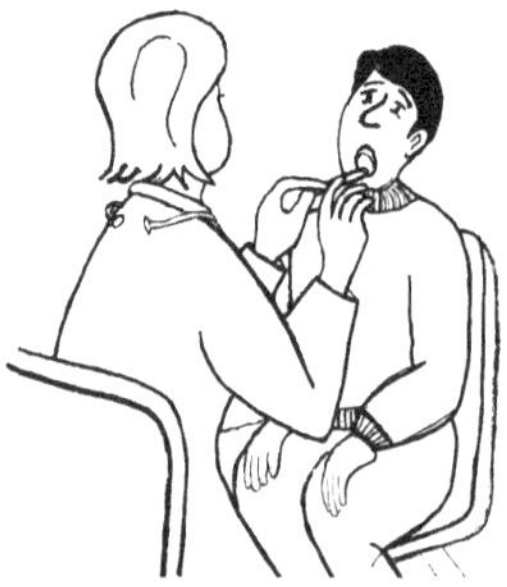

4. _ _ _ _ _ _ _ _ _ _ _ _ _ _

5. _

6. _ _ _ _ _ _ _ _ _ _ _ _ _ _ _ _ _ _ _

More medical checks

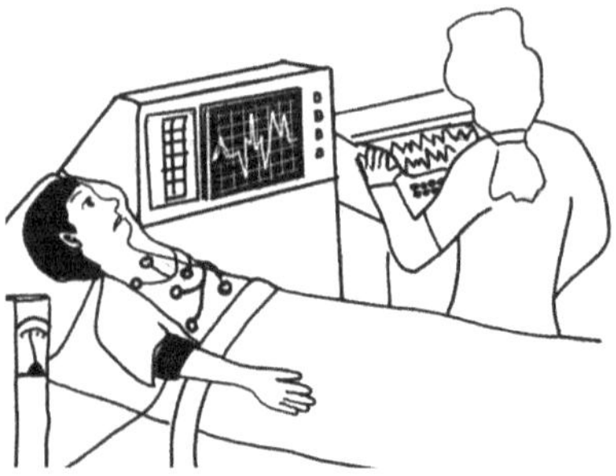

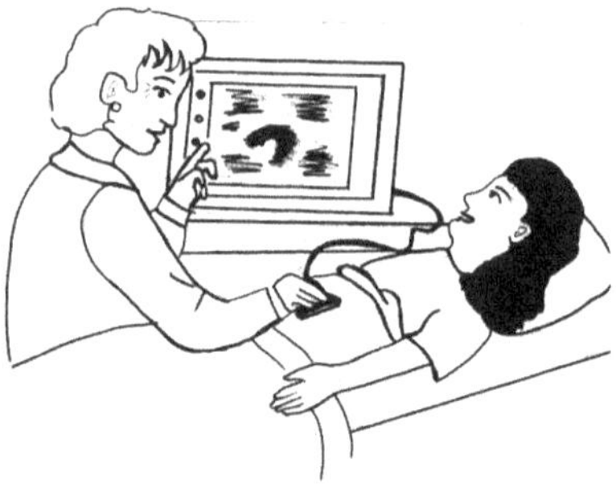

7. _ _ _

8. _ _ _ _ _ _ _ _ _ (MRI)

9. _ _ _ _ _ _ _ _ _ _

Treatments

1. tablets	2. drops	3. medicine
4. ointment	5. capsules	6. an inhaler
7. an injection	8. bandage	9. prescription

 Write

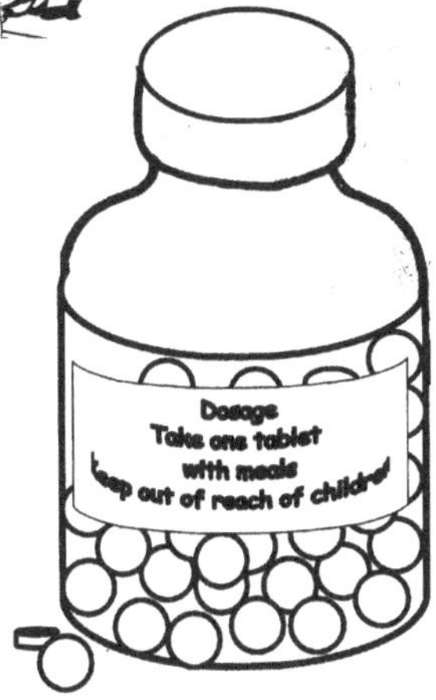

1. ________

2. ______

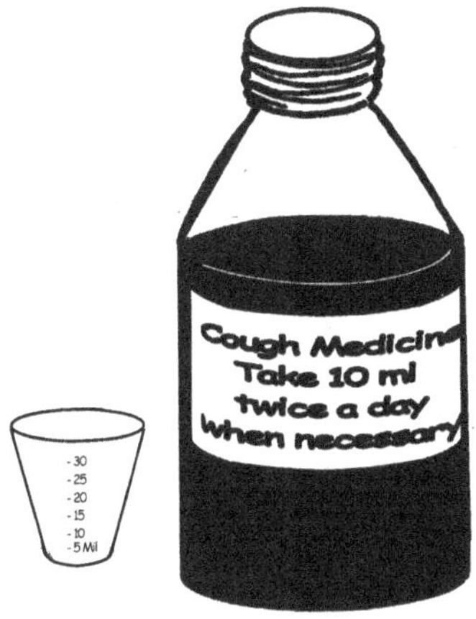

3. _________

4. ________

5. ________

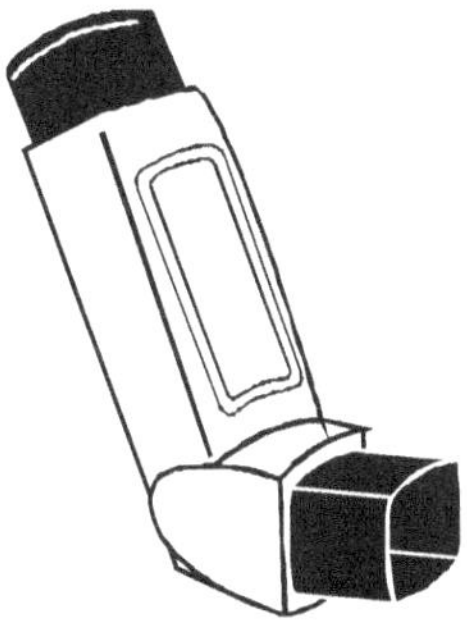

6. __ _______

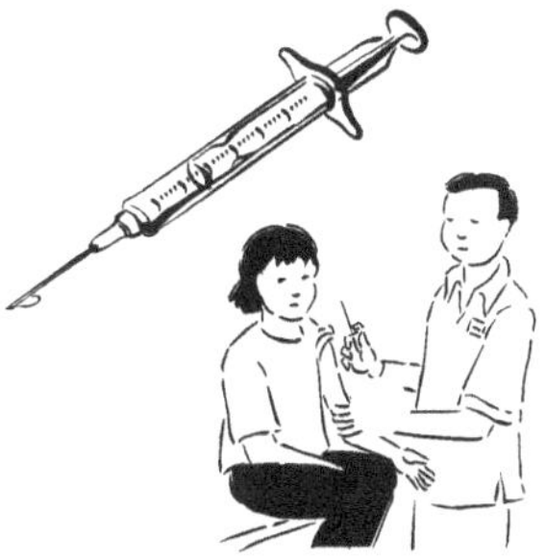

7. __ _________

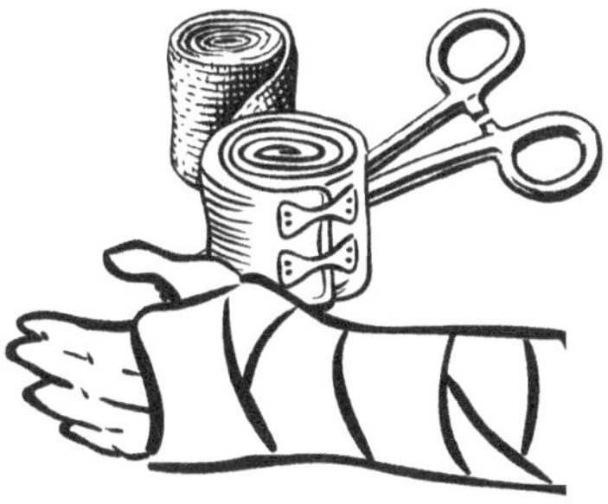

8. _______

9. ____________

More treatments

	1. exercise	2. rest
3. an IV drip	4. an operation	5. counselling
6. cast and sling		7. cast and crutches

Write

1. _ _ _ _ _ _ _ _ _

2. _ _ _ _

3. _ _ _ _ _ _ _ _

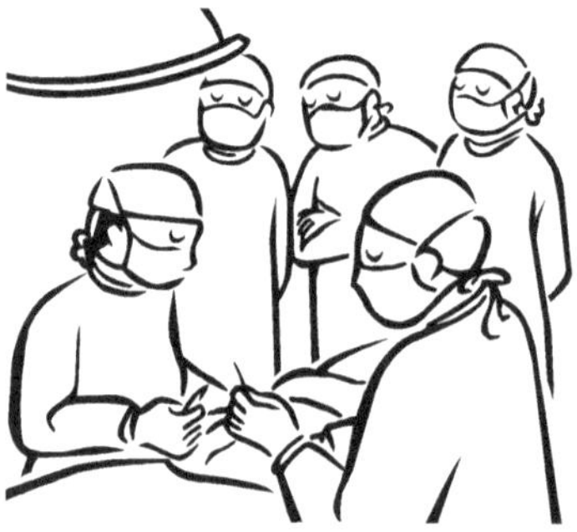

4. _ _ _ _ _ _ _ _ _ _ _

5. _ _ _ _ _ _ _ _ _

6. _ _ _ _ _ _ _ _ _ _ _ _

7. _ _ _ _ _ _ _ _ _ _ _ _ _ _ _ _

Treatments – crossword

 Write

1. 

2. 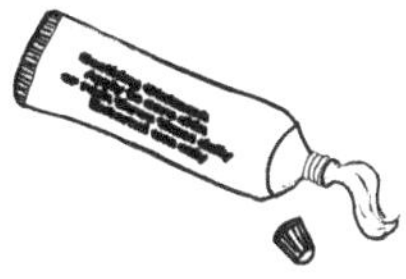

3. 

4. 

5. 

6. 

7. 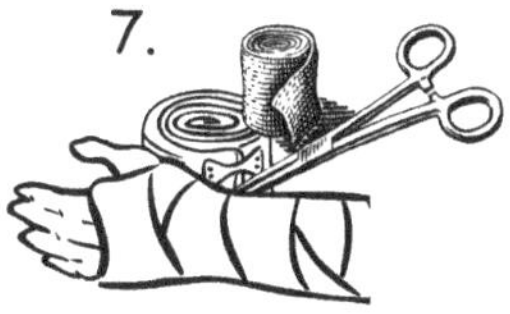

8. 

9. 

10. 

Symptoms and treatments

headache rash rest ointment

runny nose cough drops asthma inhaler

sore eye broken arm headache tablets

cast and sling broken leg cast and crutches

injection exercise back pain

sore throat medicine an operation

Write

Symptoms	Treatments

Symptoms and treatments

Write the symptom → Write the treatment

1. She has a _________.  She needs ____________________.

2. He has a ____ ___. 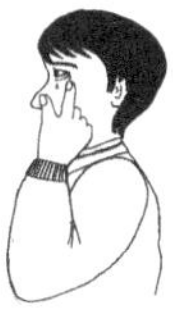 He needs ____________________.

3. He has a ____. 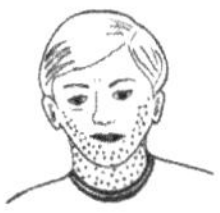 He needs ____________________.

4. He has a _____ ____ and a cough. 

He needs ____________________.

5. She has _______.  She needs an ____________________.

6. He has a _______ ___. 

He needs a _________ and _________.

7. She has a _______ ___. 

She needs a _________ and _________.

Food

	1. chicken	2. fish	3. bread	4. red meat	5. cheese
6. soup	7. noodles	8. eggs	9. rice	10. fruit	11. vegetables

Write

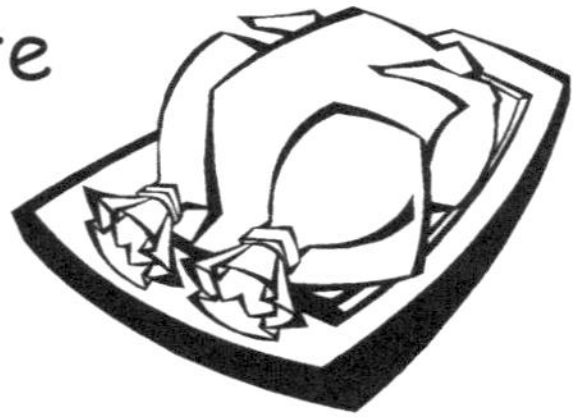

1________________ 2 ________________ 3________________ 4________________

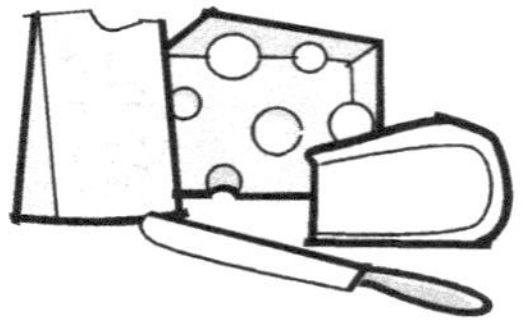

5______________ 6 ______________ 7______________ 8__________ 9__________

Write: I like ____________

10______________ 11__________________

Food crossword

Write the words from page 68 next to the numbers.

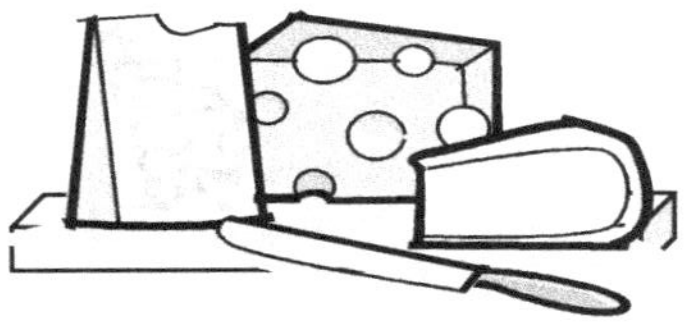

Fruit

	1. pears	2. bananas	3. watermelon	4. grapes
5. apricot	6. lemon	7. strawberries	8. apples	9. oranges
	10. pineapple	11. peach	12. cherries	

Write:

Write: I like ______________________________

Fruit

Write the words on page 70 next to the numbers.

1 p e a r s

2

3

4

5

6

7

8

9

10

11

12

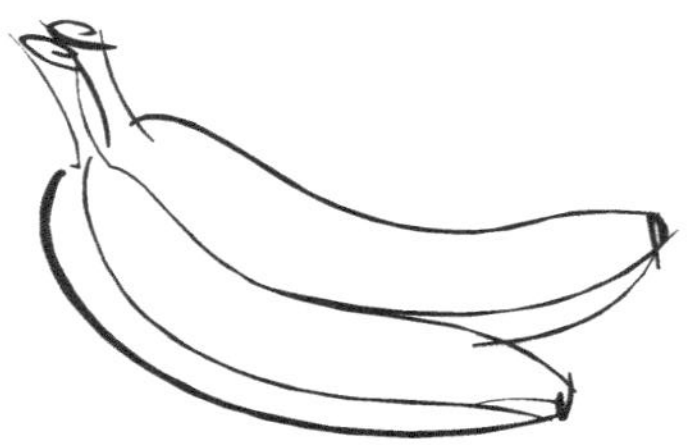

Vegetables

1. potatoes 2. corn 3. lettuce 4. carrots 5. beans
6. cabbage 7. mushrooms 8. onion 9. garlic 10. pumpkin 11. peas
12. cucumber 13. tomatoes 14. broccoli

Write

Write: I like ________________

Vegetables

Write the words next to the numbers.

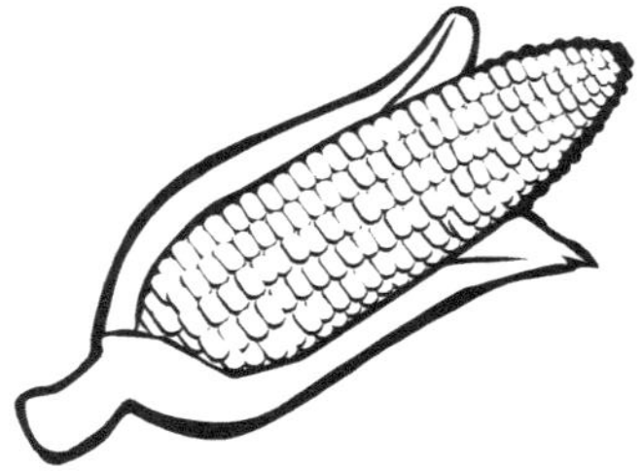

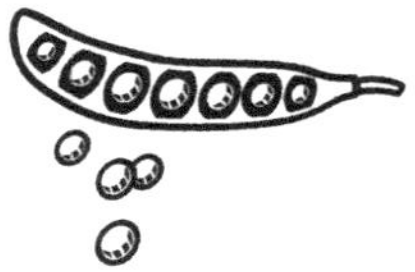

Food

peas lemons apples cheese oranges red meat
lettuce carrots bread bananas beans
fish chicken watermelon eggs tomatoes pears
broccoli corn pumpkin pineapple mushrooms

Write

Fruit	Vegetables	Other Food

What do you eat?

Write	Monday	Tuesday	Wednesday	Thursday	Friday	Saturday	Sunday
morning							
afternoon							
evening							

Staying healthy - Exercise

1. Tai Chi	2. an exercise bike	3. jogging	4. karate
5. walking	6. yoga	7. swimming	8. push-ups
9. weight-lifting	10. dancing	11. cycling	12. aerobics

Write

1. ____________________ 2. ____________________ 3. ____________________

4. ____________________ 5. ____________________ 6. ____________________

7. ____________________ 8. ____________________ 9. ____________________

10. ____________________ 11. ____________________ 12. ____________________

The best exercise for me is ____

Exercise - crossword

Write

1. 

2. 

3. 

4. 

5. 

6. 

7. 

8. 

9. 

10. 

Emergency services

1. Fire	2. Ambulance	3. Police

Write

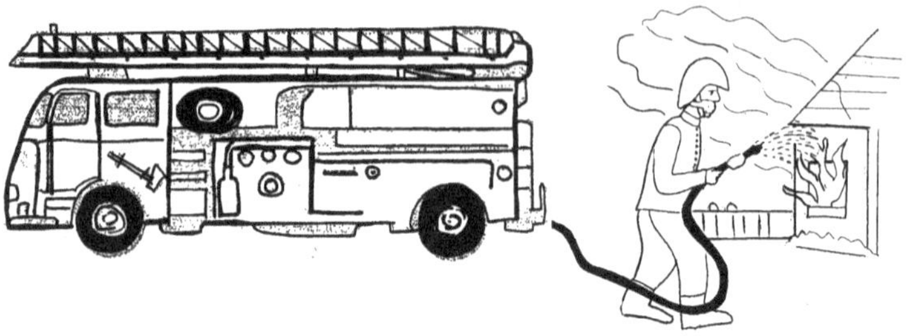

1. _ _ _ _

2. _ _ _ _ _ _ _ _ _

3. _ _ _ _ _ _

Which emergency service?

Fire, please.	Ambulance, please.	Police, please.

Write

1. ______________________

2. ______________________

3. ______________________

Emergency calls

Fire	Ambulance	Police

Write: Fire, Ambulance or Police,

1

__________ please...

2

____________ please...

3

__________ please...

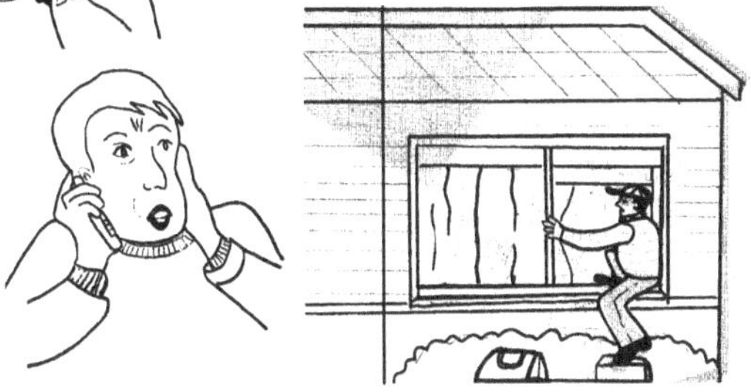

Write: Fire, Ambulance or Police.

1

_______________ please...
I think my son ate rat poison!

___________ please...
Someone took my car!

2

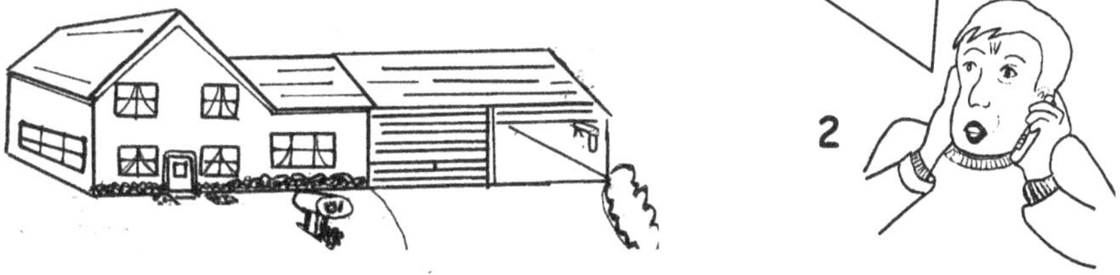

__________ please...
There is a fire in a shop.

3

Shops

1. pharmacy	2. butcher shop	3. bakery	4. hardware store
5. newsagency	6. café	7. post office	

Write

1. _ _ _ _ _ _ _ _   2. _ _ _ _ _ _ _   _ _ _ _   3. _ _ _ _ _ _

4. _ _ _ _ _ _ _ _   _ _ _ _ _   5. _ _ _ _ _ _ _ _ _ _

6. _ _ _ _   7. _ _ _ _   _ _ _ _ _ _

Where can we buy things?

Write shop names

1. We buy medicine at a ______________________________

2. We buy meat at a ______________________________

3. We buy bread at a ______________________________

4. We buy paint and tools at a ______________________________

5. We buy magazines at a ______________________________

6. We buy coffee and cake at a ______________________________

7. We buy stamps at a ______________________________

Write the shop names next to the numbers

Supermarket words

1. checkout counter	2. trolley	3. receipt
4. customer	5. groceries	6. aisle
7. shelves	8. shopping basket	9. shopping bag

Write

1. ______________ ______________ 2. ______________ 3. ______________

4. ______________ 5. ______________

6. ______________ 7. ______________

8. ______________ 9. ______________

Supermarket crossword

Write

1.

2.

3.

4.

1 2 3

4 c h e c k o u t

c o u n t e r

5

6.

6

7

8

9

5.

7.

8.

9.

Containers

1. cans 2. jars 3. bottles
4. bags 5. cartons 6. tubes 7. boxes

Write

1. _ _ _ _ 2. _ _ _ _ 3. _ _ _ _ _ _ _

4. _ _ _ _ 5. _ _ _ _ _ _ _

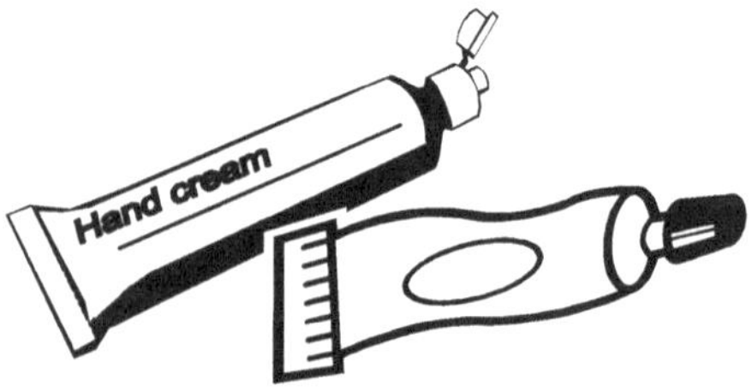

6. _ _ _ _ _ 7. _ _ _ _ _

Containers

1. can	2. jar	3. bottle	4. bag
5. carton	6. tube	7. box	

Write

1. a _ _ _ of fish 

2. a _ _ _ of jam 

3. a _ _ _ _ _ _ _ of oil 

4. a _ _ _ of nuts 

5. a _ _ _ _ _ _ _ _ of milk 

6. a _ _ _ _ of toothpaste 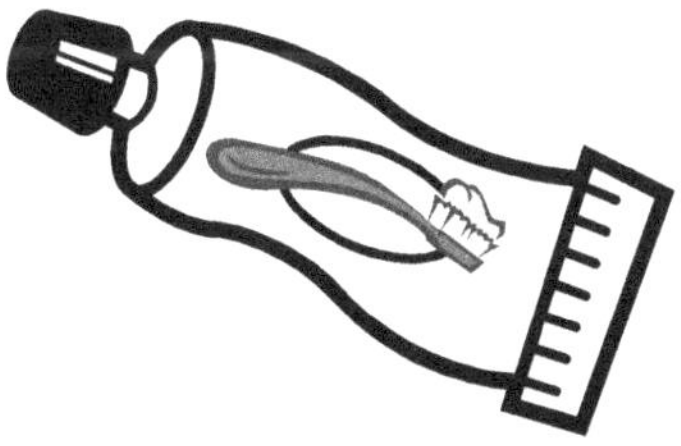

7. a _ _ _ of washing powder 

Containers

Write the container name.

1. 

2. 

3. 

4. 

5. 

6. 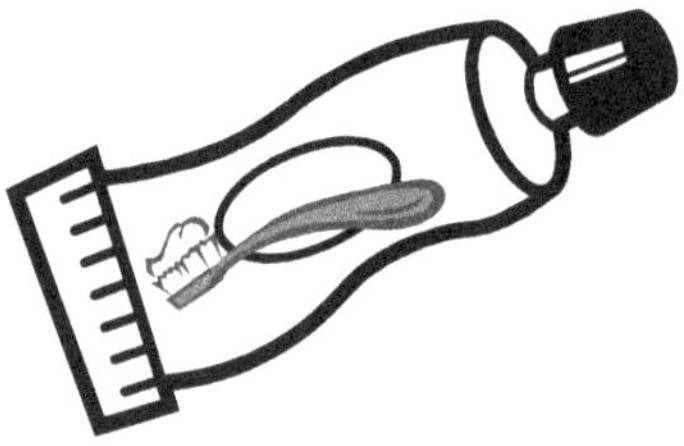

7. 

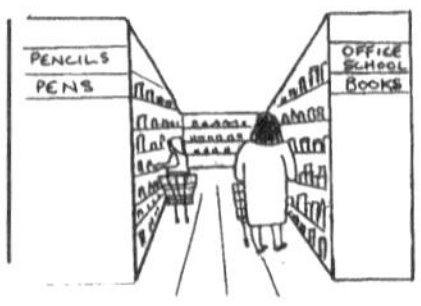

What do you buy every week?

Where is it?

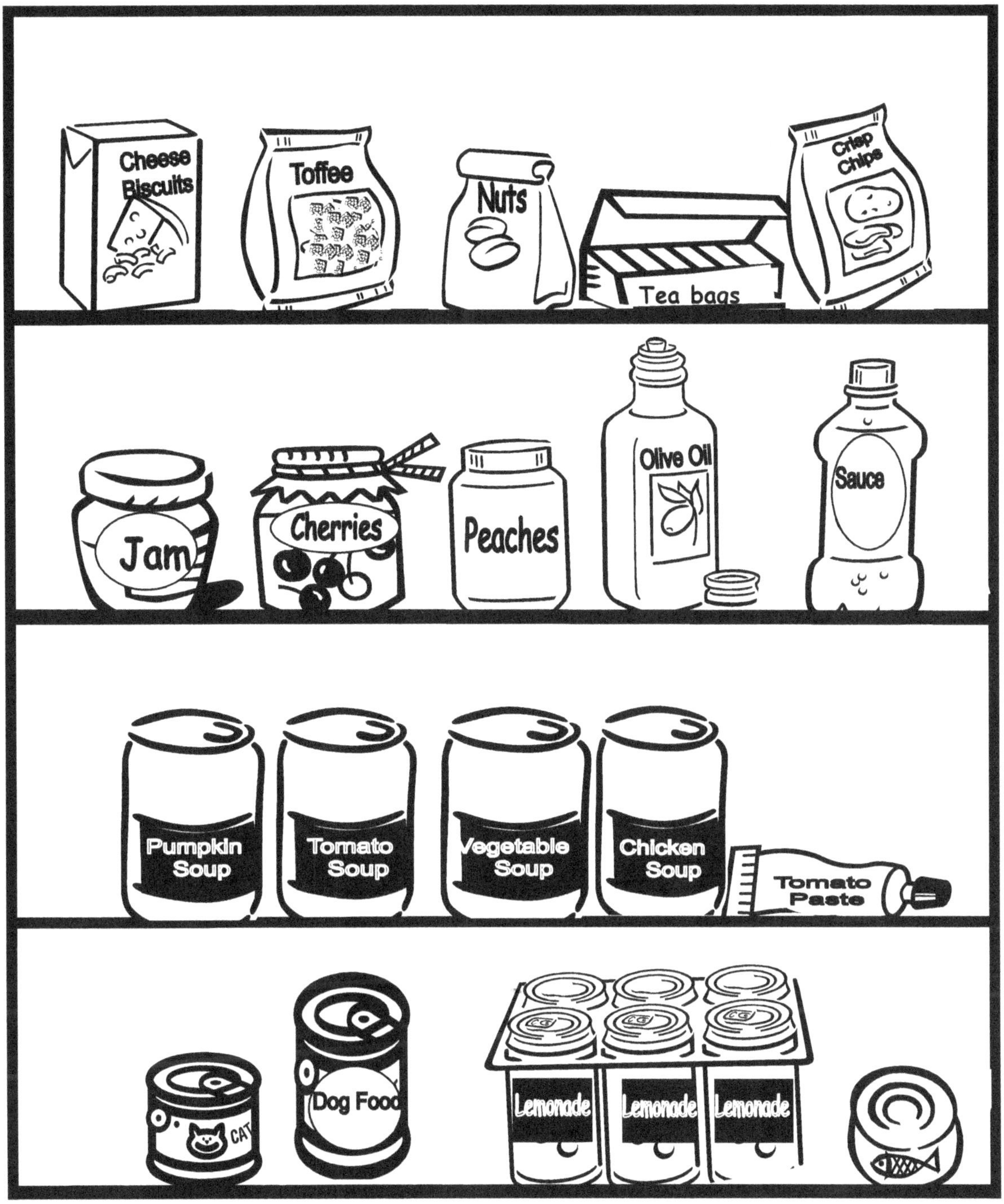

Where is the jar of peaches?

The jar of peaches is **below** the nuts.
The jar of peaches is **above** the vegetable soup.
The jar of peaches is **next to** the olive oil.
The jar of peaches is **between** the cherries and the olive oil.

Where is the tomato soup?

Write ____

Buying lunch

1. sandwich	2. salad roll	3. pizza	4. burger	5. pie
6. fried rice	7. soup	8. salad	9. fruit	

Write

1. a ________________ 2. a ________________ 3. ______________

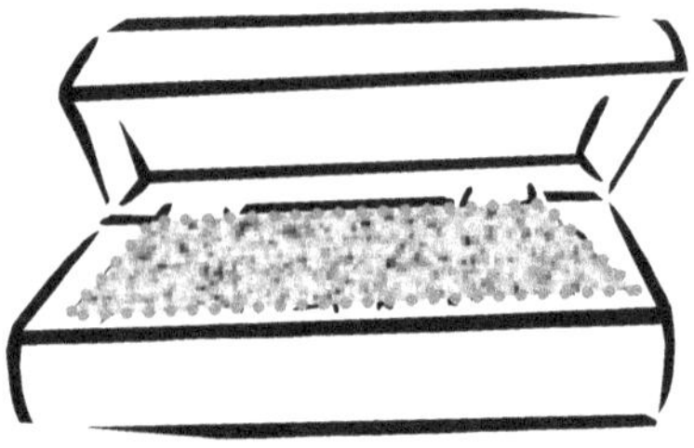

4. a __________________ 5. a ________________ 6. ______________

7. __________________ 8. _________ ______ 9. ______________

Do you buy lunch?

What do you have for lunch?

Write

I have ____for lunch.

Buying lunch

Write the words next to the numbers

1. 

2. 

3. 

4. 

5. 

6. 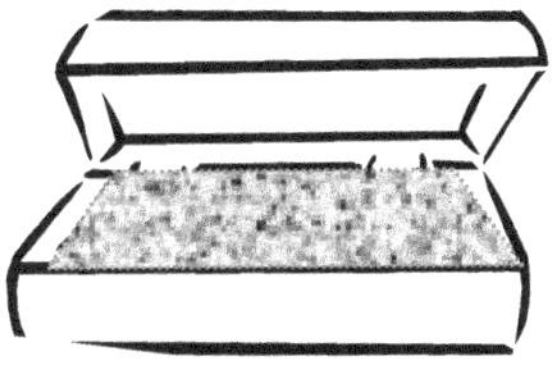

7. 

8. 

9. 

When we buy lunch, we say:

I'd like ________________________________ please.

At the pharmacy

1. medicine	2. a prescription	3. ointment	4. sunscreen
5. perfume	6. drops	7. cosmetics	8. tablets

 Write

1.____________________ 2.____________________ 3.____________________

4.____________________ 5.____________________ 6.____________________

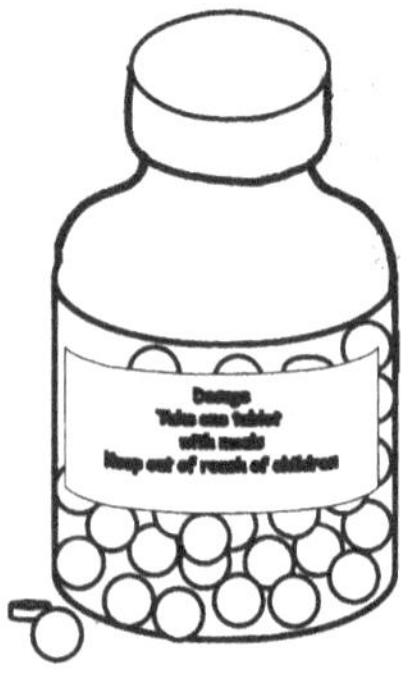

7.____________________________ 8.________________________

At the pharmacy

Write the words next to the numbers.

1.

2.

3.

4

```
          1
          m
2  a [ ]   e
          d
   3       i
          c
      4   i
   5       n
          e
6                     8
      7
```

5.

6.

7.

8.

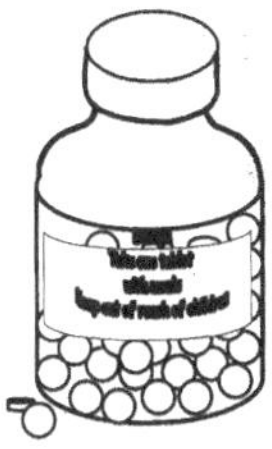

Things in the kitchen

1. kettle 2. toaster 3. teapot 4. saucepan

5. frying pan 6. plate 7. mug 8. cup and saucer

9. bowl 10. spoon 11. knife 12. fork

Write

1. ____________ 2. ________________ 3. ________________

4. ____________________ 5. ________________ __________

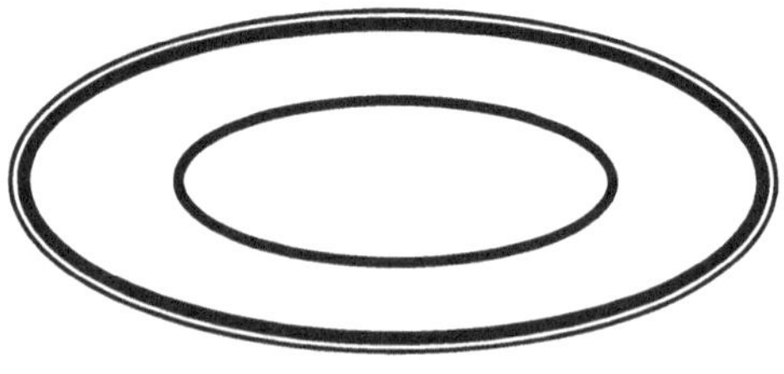

6. ______________ 7. __________________

8. __________ and ______________

Things in the kitchen

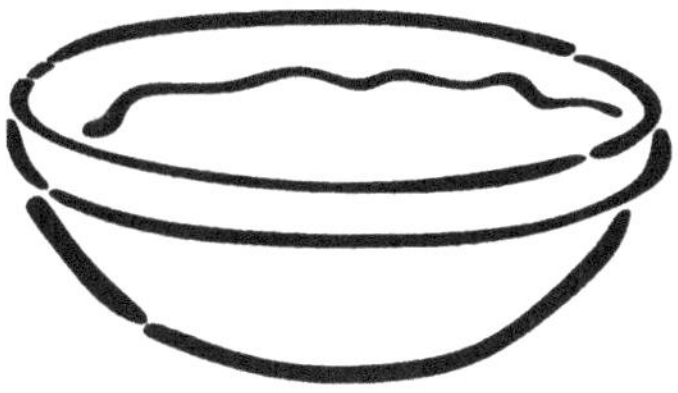

9. ____________ 10. ____________ 11. ____________ 12. ____________

Write the words next to the numbers.

At the electrical store

1. washing machine	2. microwave	3. vacuum cleaner
4. sound system	5 iron 6. stove	7. television
8. fan	9. fridge	10. coffee machine

Write

1. ______________ 2. __________________ 3. __________________

4. ________ ________ 5. __________________ 6. __________________

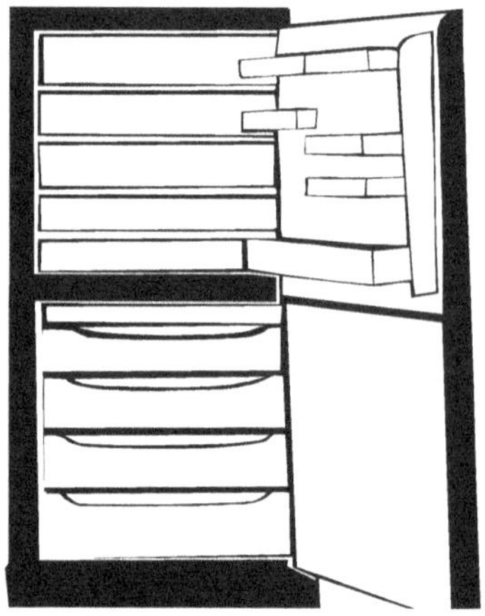

7. _______________ 8. ___________ 9. _____________ 10. ___________

____

Electrical store - crossword

Write

1.

2.

3.

4.

5.

6.

7.

8.

9.
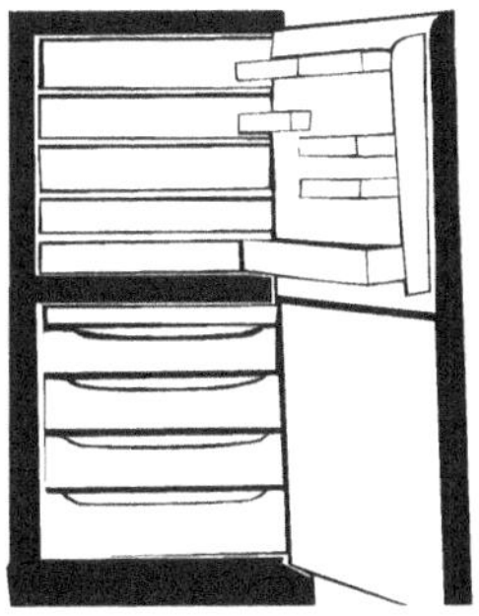

10.

At the hardware store

1. electric drill 2. hammer 3. screwdriver 4. spanner

5. paint 6. spade 7. ladder

8. rake 9. wheelbarrow 6. paint brushes

Write

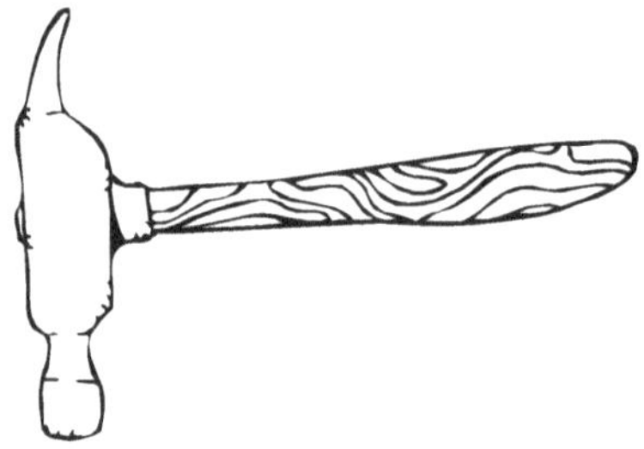

1. ______________ 2. __________________ 3. __________________

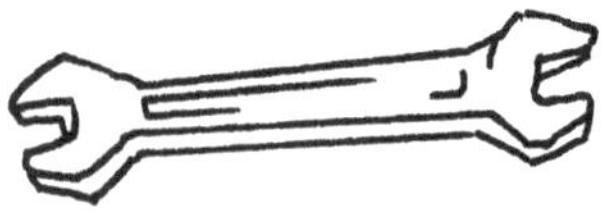

4. _______ ________ 5. __________________ 6. __________________

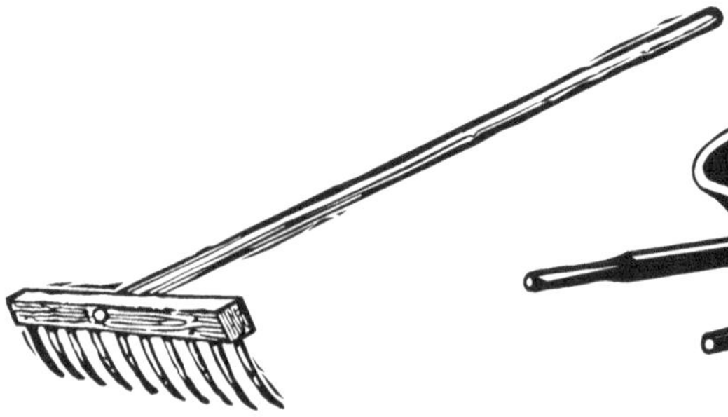

7. ______________ 8. _____________________ 9. __________________

10. _________________________

Hardware store - crossword

Write

1. 

2. 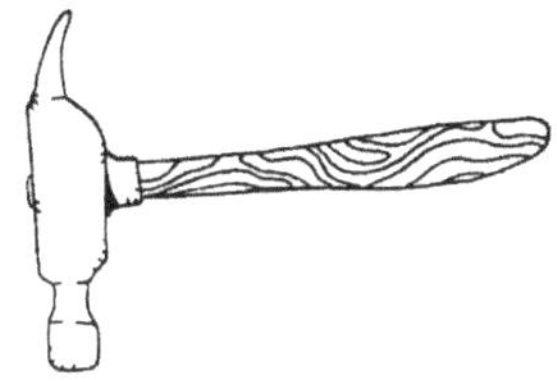

3. 

4. 

5. 

6. 

1 e l e c t r i c d r i l l

7. 

8. 

9. 

At the furniture store

1. chairs 2. table 3. drawers 4. armchair
5. sofa 6. coffee table 7. bookcase 8. desk
9. cupboard 10. stool 11. single bed 12. double bed

Write

1. ______________

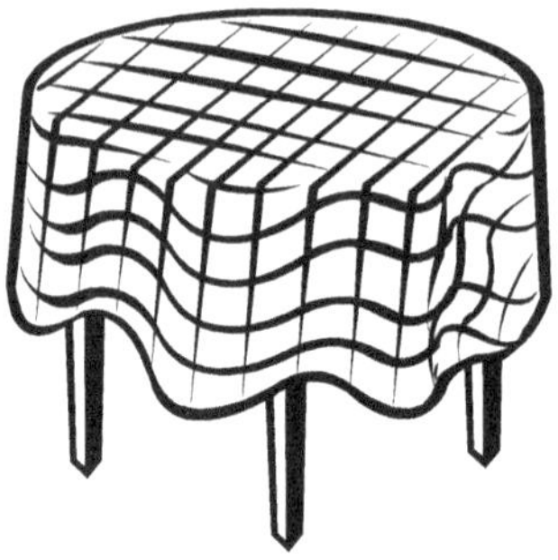

2. __________________

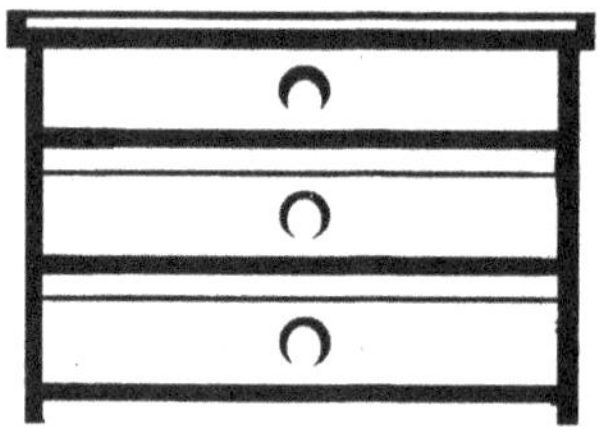

3. __________________

4. ______________

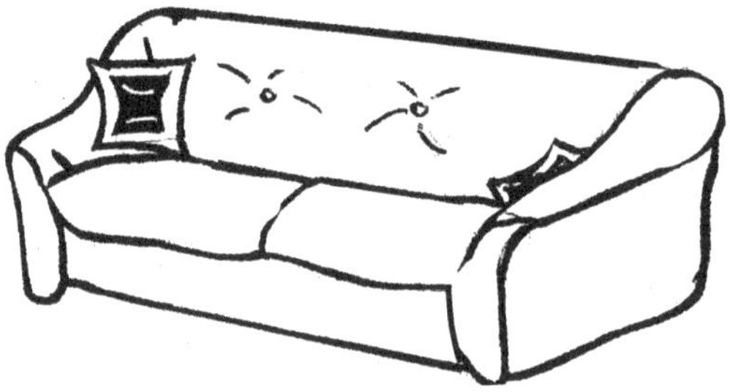

5. __________________

6. _____________ ________

7. ________________

8. __________________

9. __________________________

At the furniture store

10. ______________ 11. ____________ ________ 9. ______________ _________

Write the words next to the numbers

Where can we buy things?

sofa	washing machine	single bed	medicine	hammer
	vacuum cleaner	television	perfume	
paint brushes	prescription	microwave	ladder	
table	armchair	drops	screwdriver	

Write

Furniture store	Electrical store
Hardware store	**Pharmacy**

Where can we find things at home?

armchair	toaster	sofa	fridge	saucepan	cupboard
stove	drawers	coffee machine		wheelbarrow	kettle
rake	microwave		coffee table	bed	spade

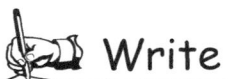

 Write

Kitchen	Bedroom
Living room	**Garden**

Transport

train	bicycle	bus	plane	taxi
tram	on foot	car	motorbike	boat

Write

1. by ______________

2. by ________________

3. by __________________

4. by _______________

5. by _______________

6. by _____________

7. ___ ________________

8. by ______________

9. by __________________

Write

10. by _______________

I go to the shopping centre ______________

____

Transport - crossword

Write the words next to the numbers.

1. 

2. 

3. 

1 t r a i n

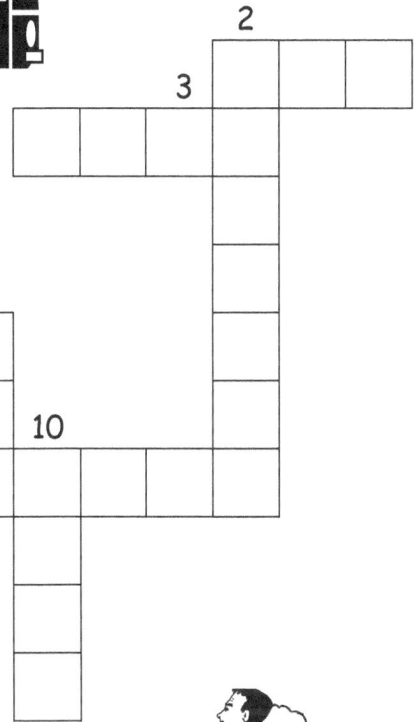

2 3 4 5 6 7 8 9 10

4. 

5. 

6. 

7. 

8. 

9. 

10. 

Places

1. post office	2. school	3. swimming pool	
4. hospital	5. train station	6. library	7. gym
8. cinema	9. bank		

Write

1. ________ ________ 2. ______________ 3. ______________ _____

4. ______________ 5. __________________ 6. ________________

7. ______________ 8. ________________ 9. ________________

Places crossword

Write the words next to the numbers.

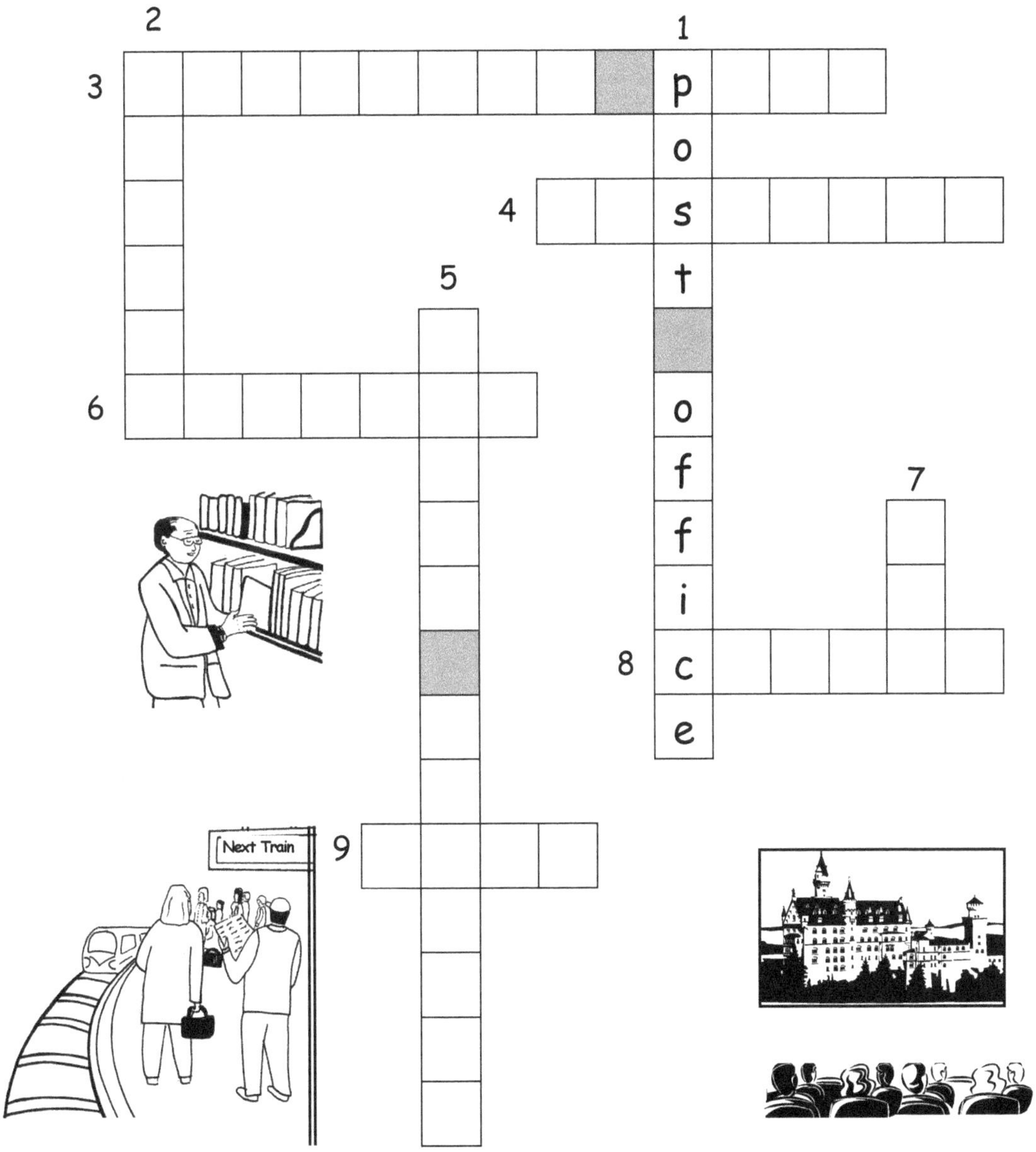

Train travel

1. timetable	2. platform	3. ticket
4. ticket office	5. ticket gate	6. ticket slot

Write

Trains to:	Depart at:	Platform
City Central	11.30 am	1
Katoomba	11.45	2
Parramatta	12.30	3

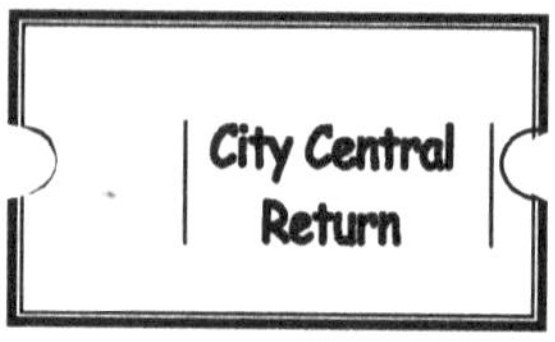

1. ____________________ 2. ____________________ 3. ____________________

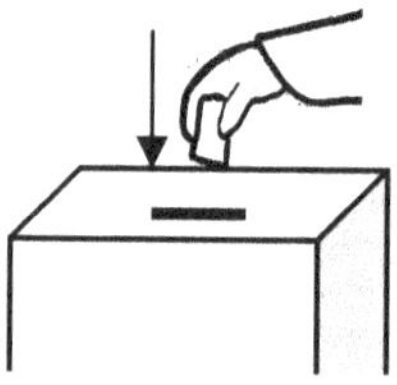

4. __________ __________ 5. __________ __________ 6. __________ __________

Write the words next to the numbers.

Word lists

plumber sandwich shirt strawberries boat
mechanic coat nurse
soup motorbike painter jeans
plane skirt hairdresser rice
cheese jacket chef train

Write the words in the correct list.

Food	Clothes

Jobs	Transport

Answers

Name and Address, page 9

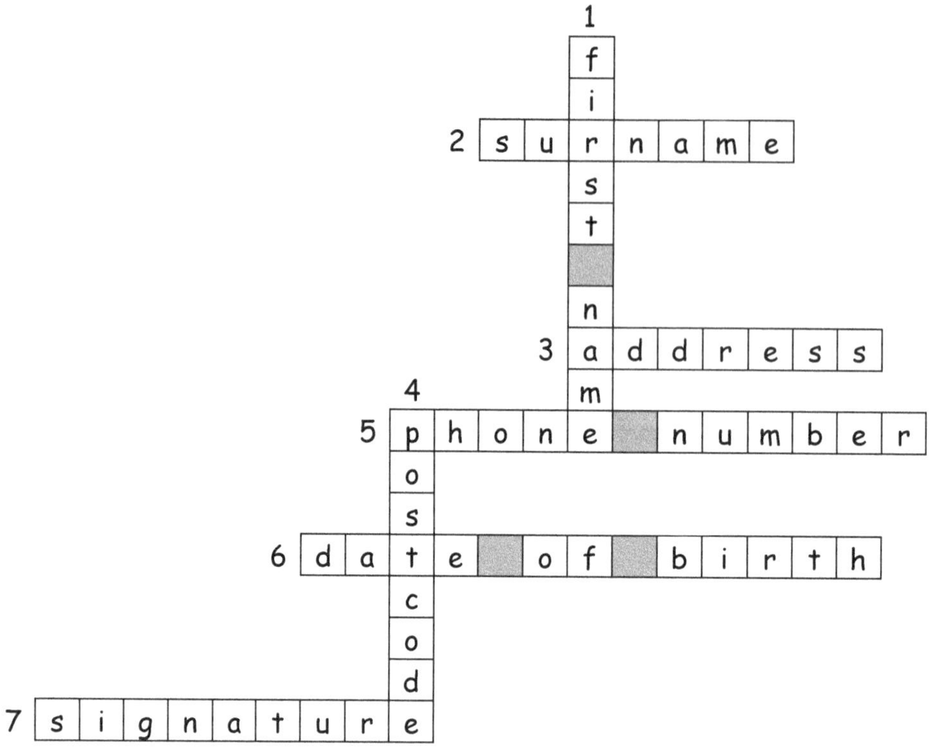

page 10

1. 80 Main Street
   Summerton

2. 55 Short Avenue
   Summerton

3. Unit 2, 326 King Road
   Summerton

Things in the classroom, page 17

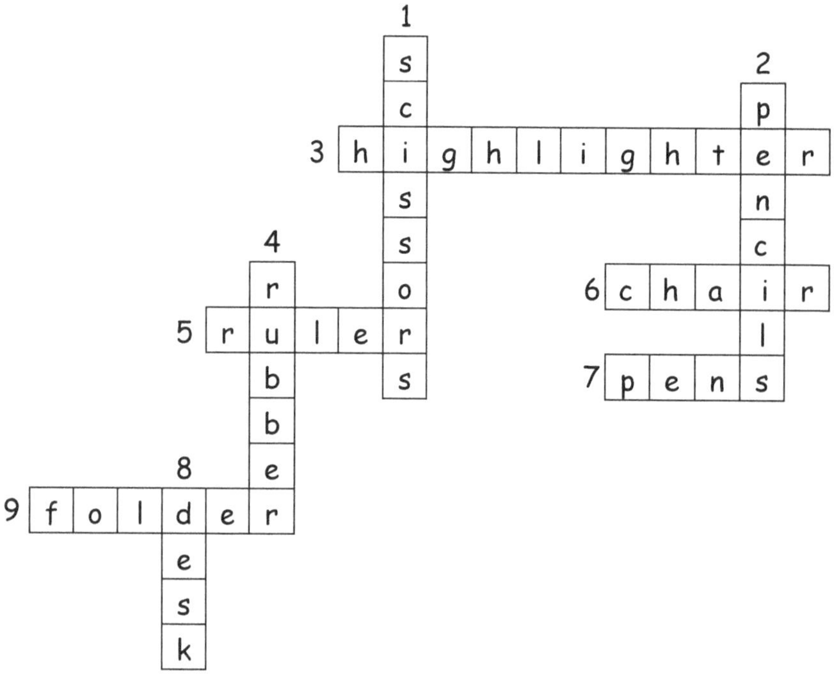

Days of the week, page 18

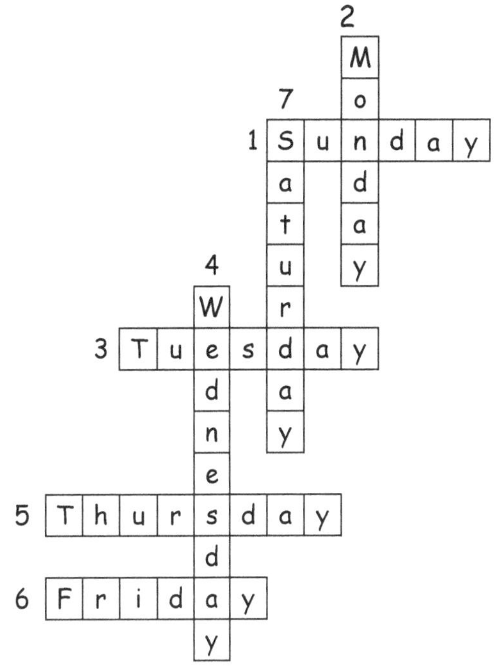

1. Sunday
2. Monday
3. Tuesday
4. Wednesday
5. Thursday
6. Friday
7. Saturday

What is the time? page 20

10.15	It is ten fifteen.	(or It is fifteen minutes past ten.)
6.20	It is six twenty.	(or It is twenty minutes past six.)
8.00	It is eight o'clock.	

What is the time? page 21

5.00	It is five o'clock.	
9.30	It is nine thirty.	(or It is half past nine.)
10.10	It is ten ten.	(or It is ten minutes past ten.)
6.50	It is six fifty.	(or It is ten to seven.)

Plural words, page 23

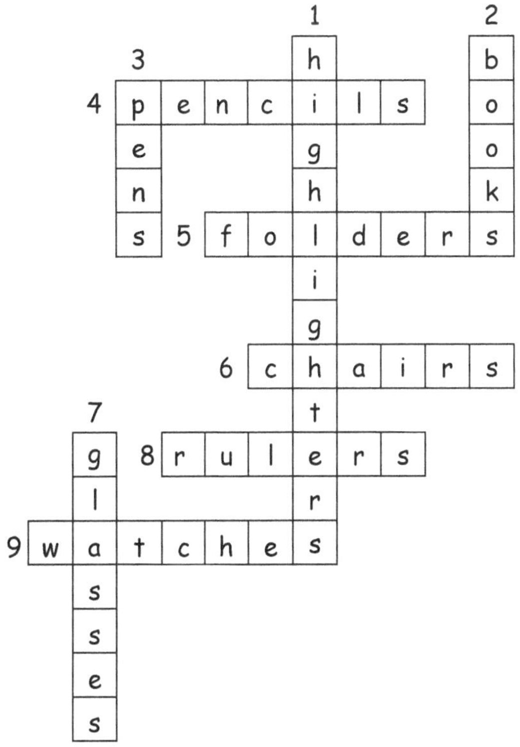

Road signs, page 25

1. go left	2. go right
3. do not go left	4. do not go right
5. do not go here	6. No U turn - do not turn around
7. walk	8. don't walk

Signs, page 26

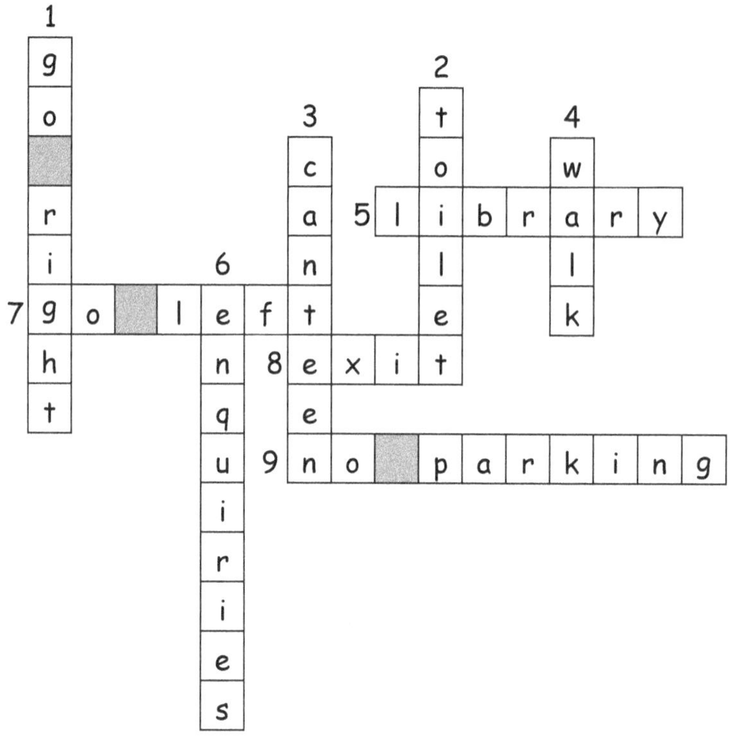

Directions, page 27

1. Go left 2. Go right 3. Go straight ahead
4. Turn left 5. Turn right 6. Turn and go back 7. Turn and go back

People, page 29

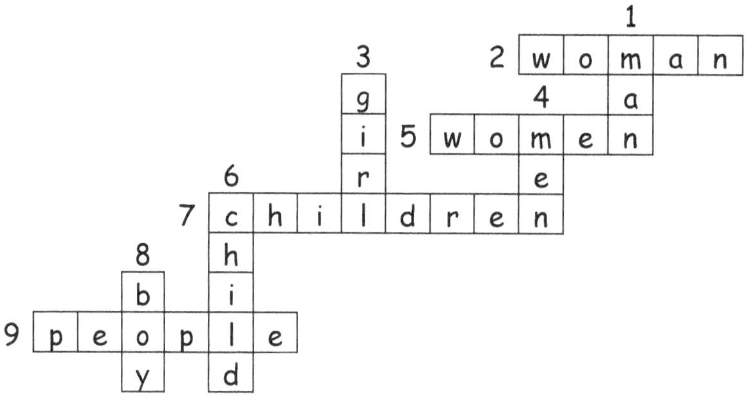

Family, page 30

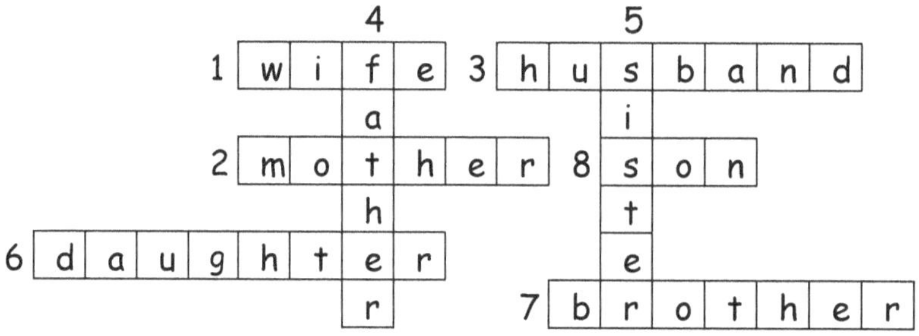

Talking aboutme and other people, page 32

1. This is my family. 2. This is my son. 3. He is eleven years old.
4. This is my daughter. 5. She is twelve years old.
6. This is my mother-in- law (7.) and father-in-law. 8. They live near my house.
9. This is my friend. 10. She comes from South America.

Face, page 33

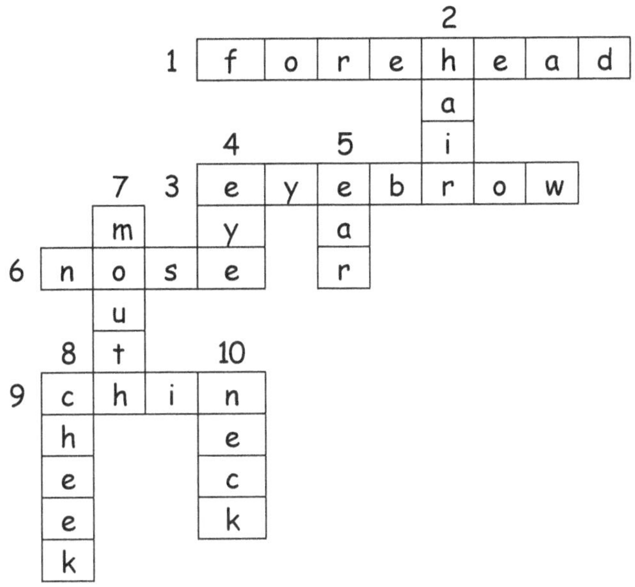

Clothes, page 37

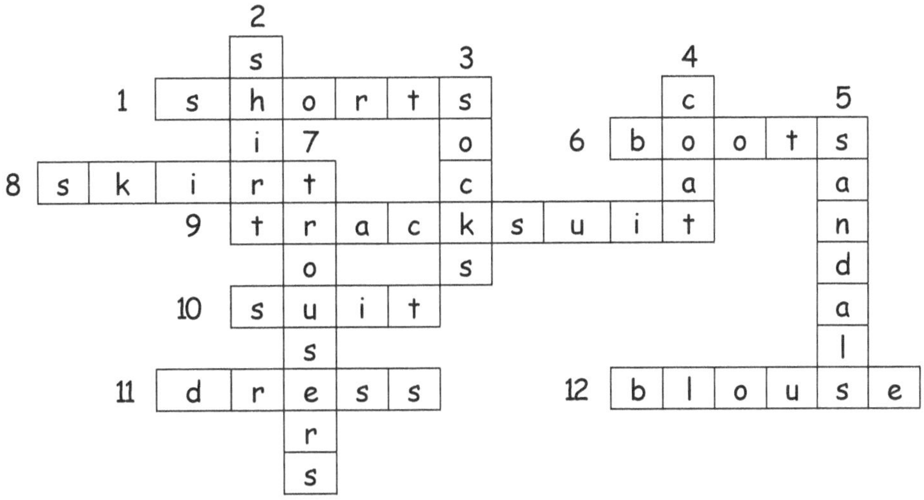

Describing people, page 39

Jong is wearing a jumper and a shirt and a tie and trousers and shoes.

Lee is wearing a shirt and a tie and a suit and a belt.

Wei is wearing a dress and sandals.

Activities, page 42

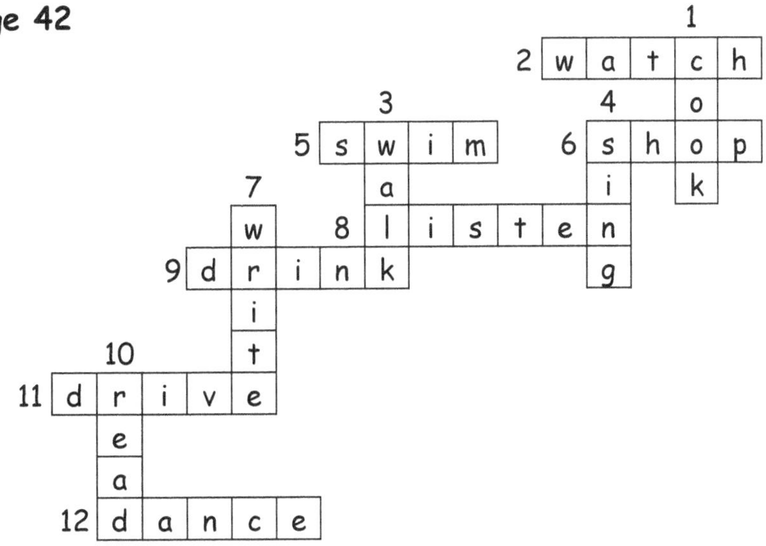

Sport, page 45

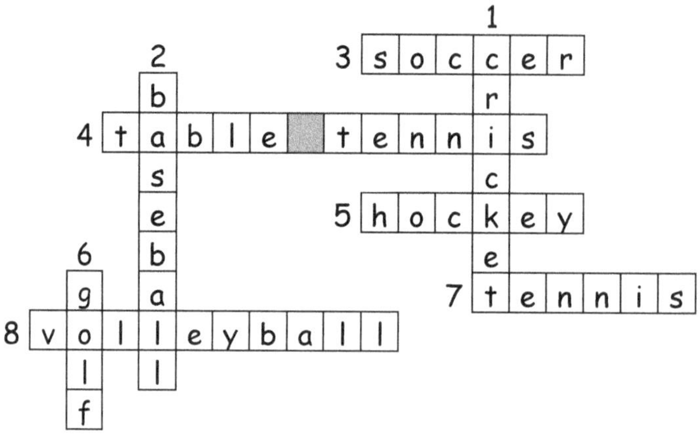

Jobs, page 47

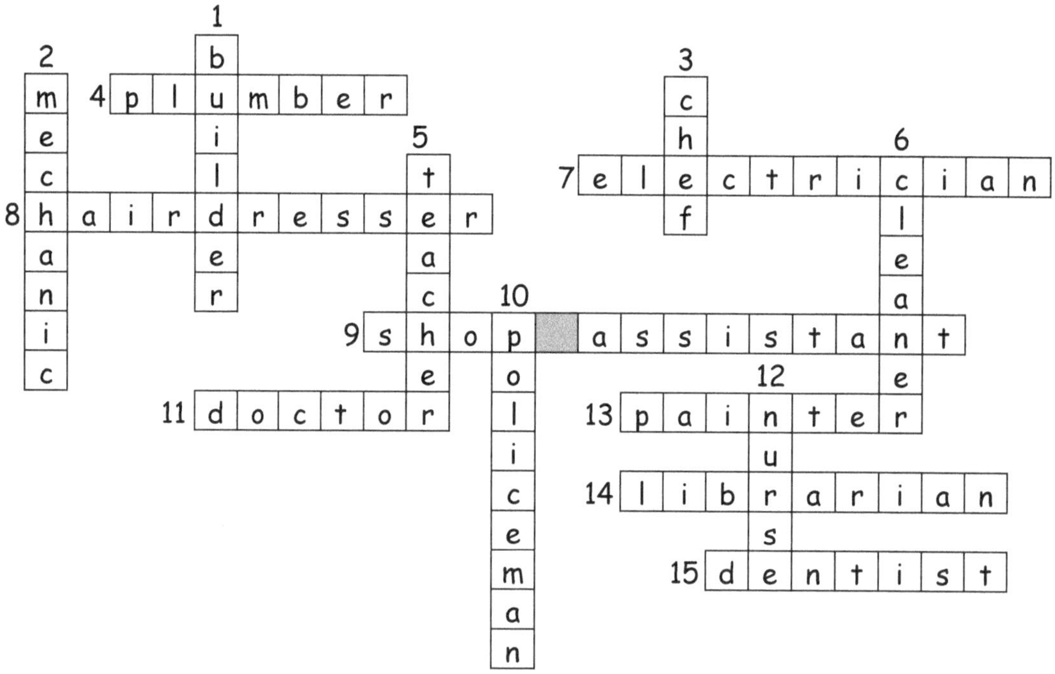

Seasons of the year, page 49

Australia, New Zealand, South America, South Africa (Southern hemisphere)

Summer December January February	**Autumn** March April May
Winter June July August	**Spring** September October November

Europe, USA, UK, etc (Northern hemisphere)

Summer June July August	**Autumn** September October November
Winter December January February	**Spring** March April May

Daily Routine, page 51

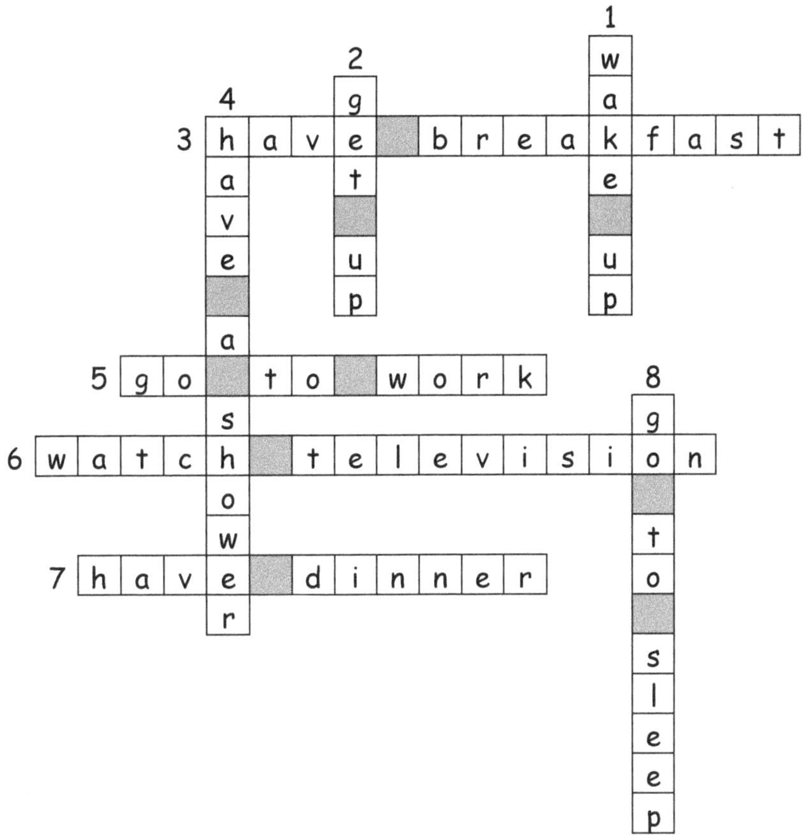

Special Days, page 52

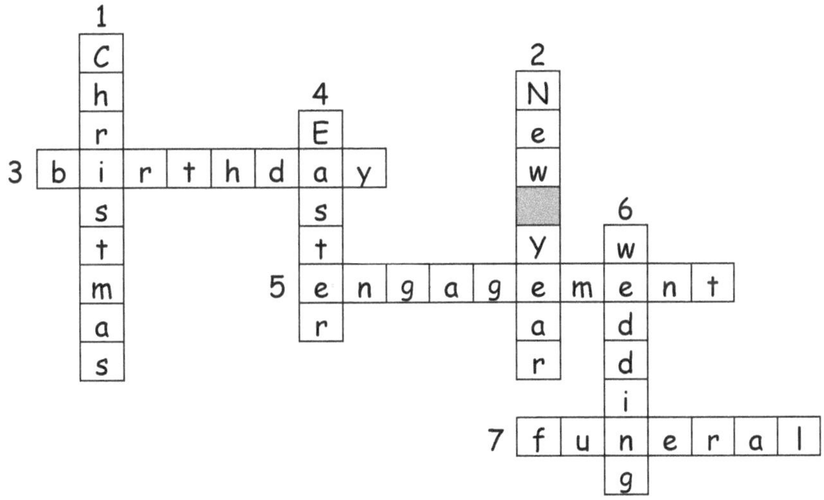

Special cards for special days, page 53

1. Christmas
2. New Year
3. birthday
4. Easter
5. engagement
6. wedding
7. funeral

Past, present and future time, page 54

past time	present time	future time
yesterday did last month last year	now at present	tomorrow next month next year will

Past time, page 55

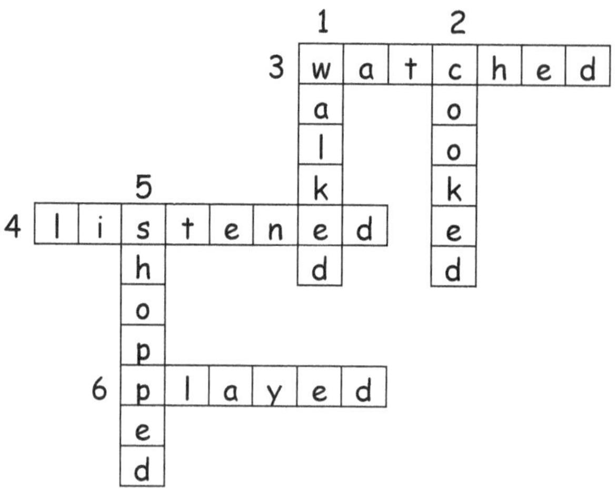

More past tense verbs, page 56

1. Yesterday was hot.
2. I went to the supermarket yesterday.
3. I did my homework last night.
4. I saw a kangaroo last week.
5. Yesterday I bought new shoes.
6. We came to this country last year.

Past and future, page 57

Yesterday I walked in the park.
Yesterday I cooked chicken.
Yesterday I watched TV.
Yesterday I listened to music.
Yesterday I shopped for food.
Yesterday I talked to my friend.
Yesterday I played cards.

Tomorrow I will walk in the park.
Tomorrow I will cook chicken.
Tomorrow I will watch TV.
Tomorrow I will listen to music.
Tomorrow I will shop for food.
Tomorrow I will talk to my friend.
Tomorrow I will play cards.

Health - Parts of the body, page 59

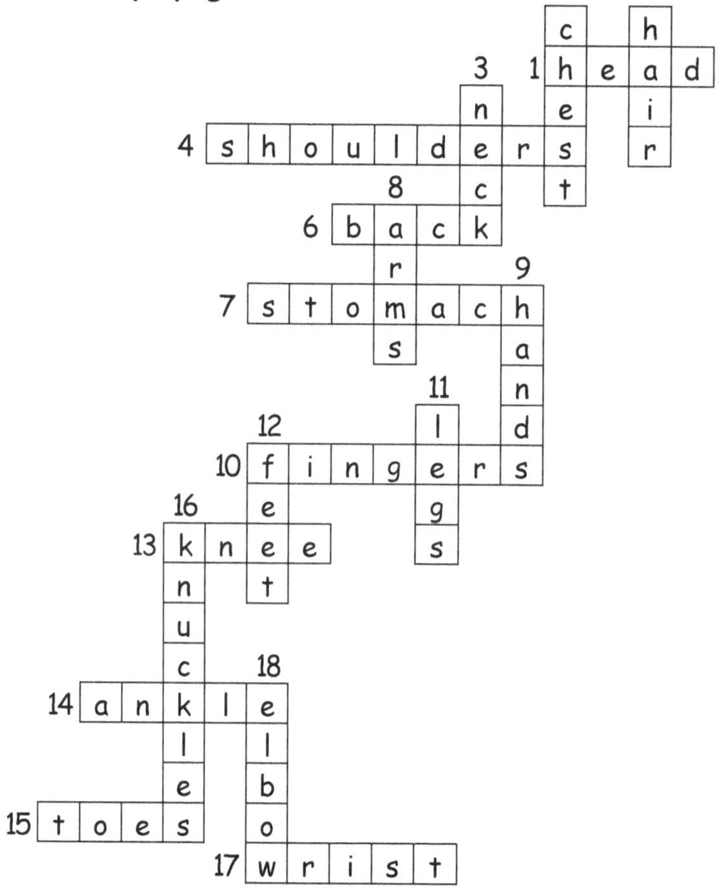

Symptoms, page 61

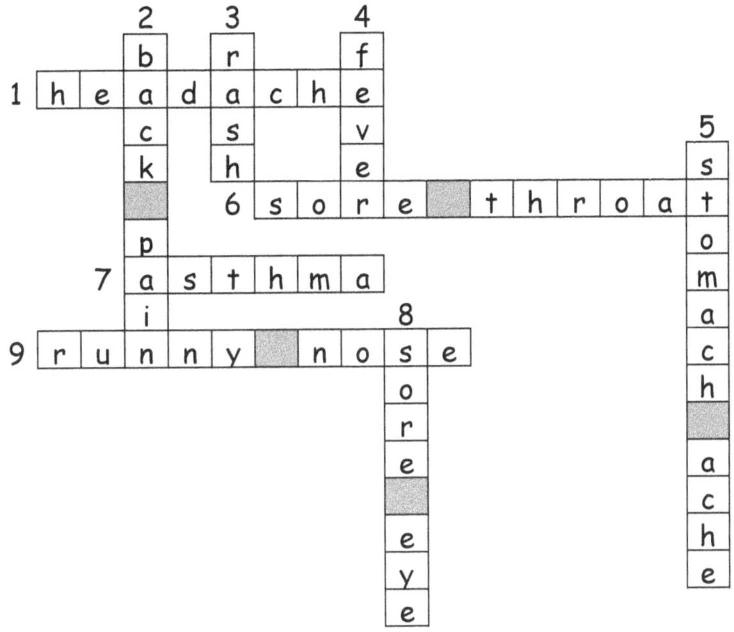

Treatment crossword, page 65

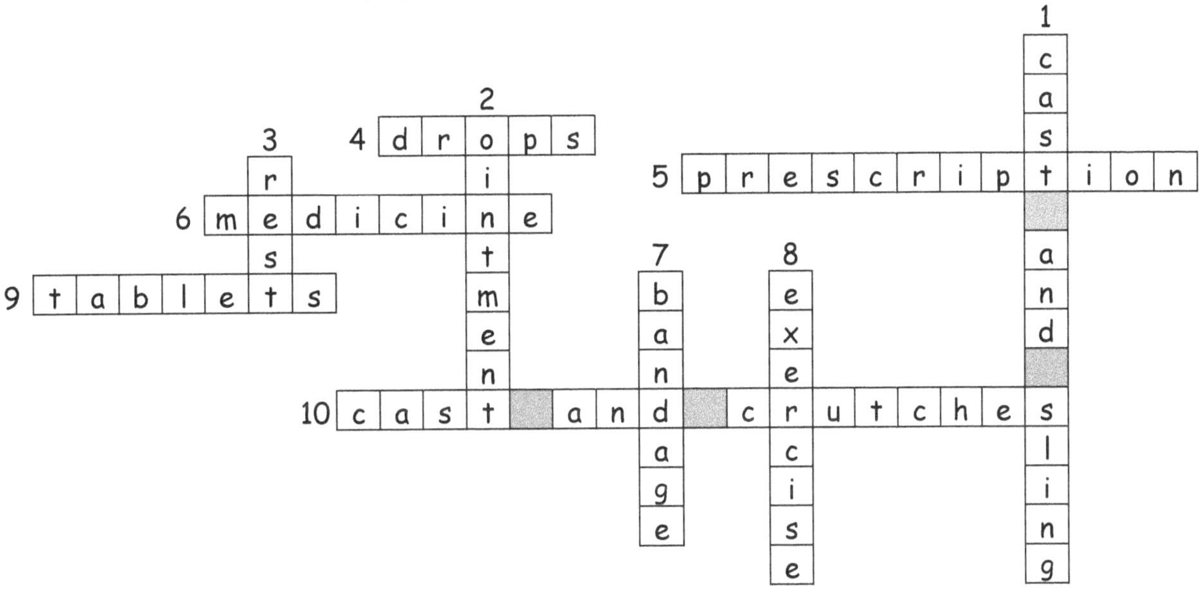

Symptoms and treatment, page 66

Symptoms		Treatment		
headache	sore eye	rest	headache tablets	drops
rash	broken arm	ointment	cast and sling	medicine
runny nose	broken leg	inhaler	cast and crutches	injection
cough	asthma	exercise	an operation	medicine
back pain	sore throat			

Symptoms and treatment, page 67

1. She has a headache.	She needs headache tablets (and rest).
2. He has a sore eye.	He needs drops.
3. He has a rash.	He needs ointment.
4. He has a runny nose and a cough.	He needs medicine.
5. She has asthma.	She needs an inhaler.
6. He has a broken arm.	She needs a cast and sling.
7. She has a broken leg.	She needs a cast and crutches.

Food, page 69

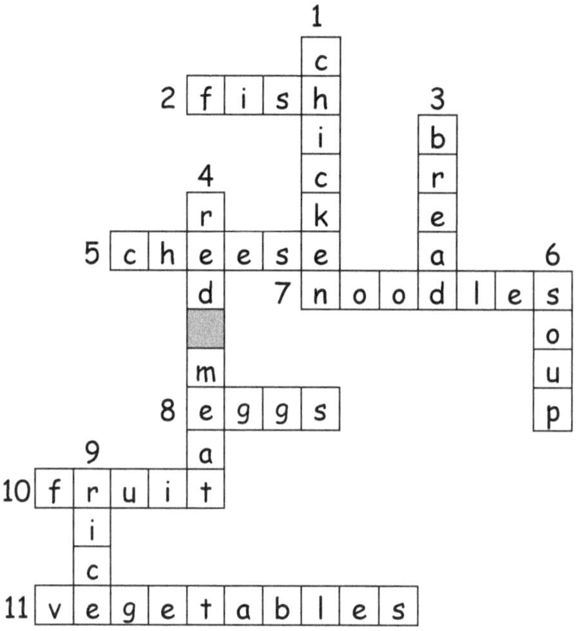

Fruit, page 71

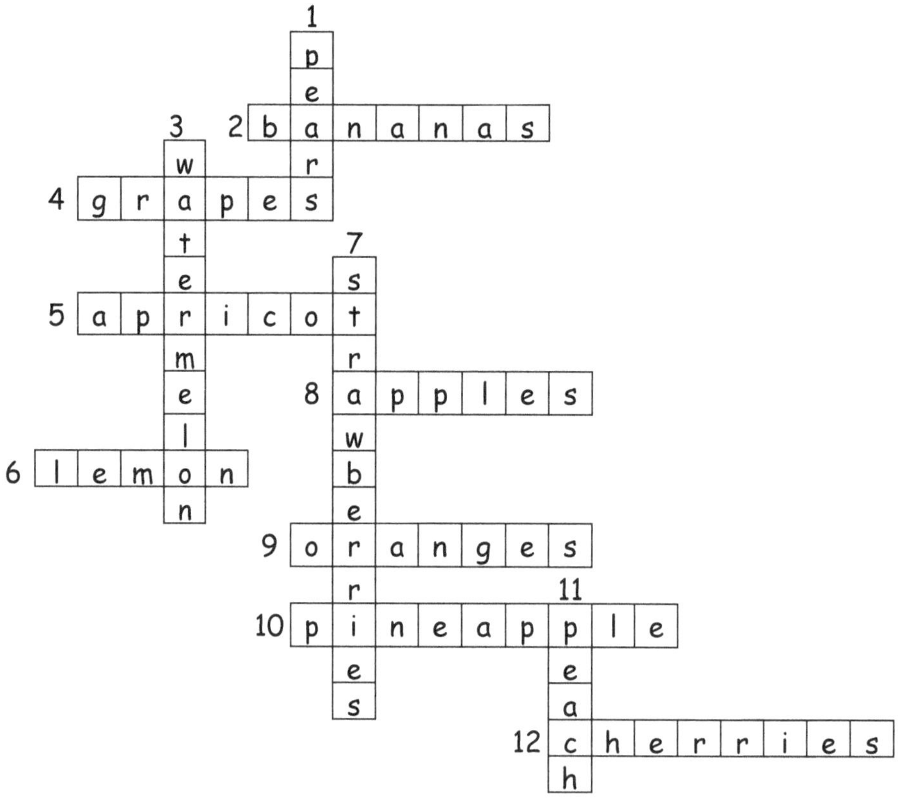

Food, page 74

Fruit	Vegetables	Other food
lemons apples oranges bananas watermelon pears pineapple	peas lettuce carrots beans tomatoes broccoli corn pumpkin mushrooms	cheese red meat bread fish chicken eggs

Vegetables, page 73

```
                                      1
                                      p
                                      o                    2
                         3  l  e  t  t  u  c  e
                                      a                    o
                   4  c  a  r  r  o  t  s             r
                5                    o                     n
             6  c  a  b  b  a  g  e
                      e                    s
                      a
                      n                    8
             7  m  u  s  h  r  o  o  m  s
                            n
                   9  g  a  r  l  i  c
                                      o
                               10     n
                         11  p  e  a  s
                               u
                   12  c  u  c  u  m  b  e  r
                   13                 p
                         t            k
          14  b  r  o  c  c  o  l  i
                         m            n
                         a
                         t
                         o
                         e
                         s
```

Exercise, page 77

```
                      1
          2  t  a  i     c  h  i
                   e
                   r                    3
                   o                    j
                   b                    o
          4  s  w  i  m  m  i  n  g
                   c                    g
                   s                    i
                         5              n
                      6  w  e  i  g  h  t  -  l  i  f  t  i  n  g
                         a
                         l
                      7  k  a  r  a  t  e
                         i
                8        n
          9  c  y  c  l  i  n  g
                o
                g
          10  d  a  n  c  i  n  g
```

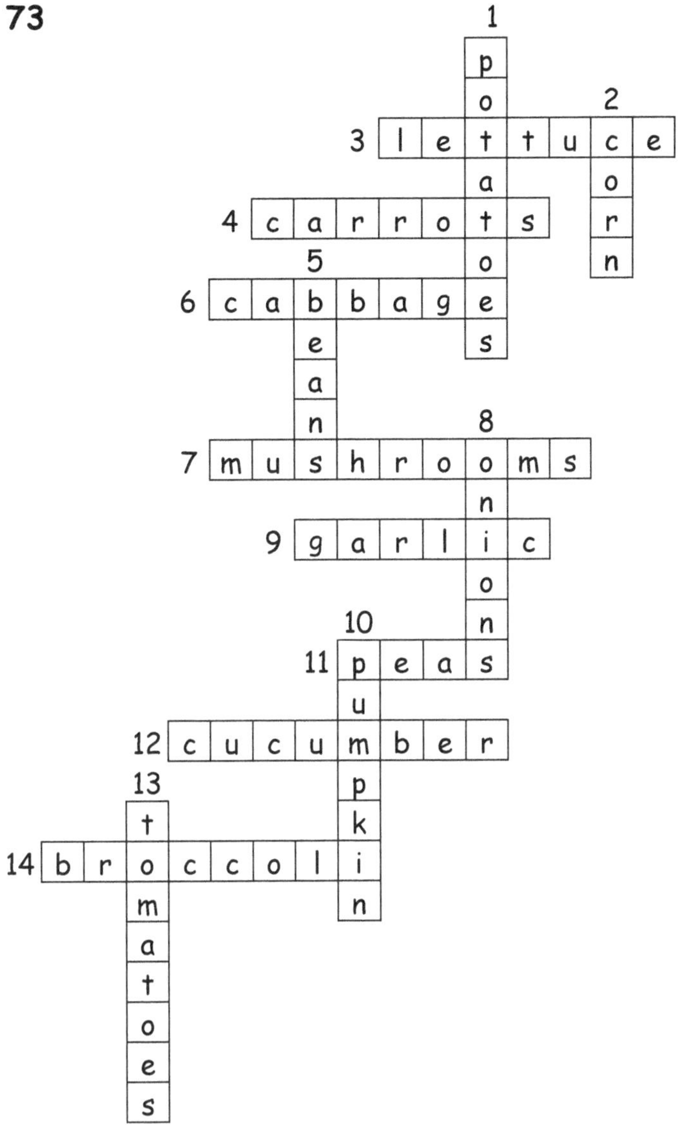

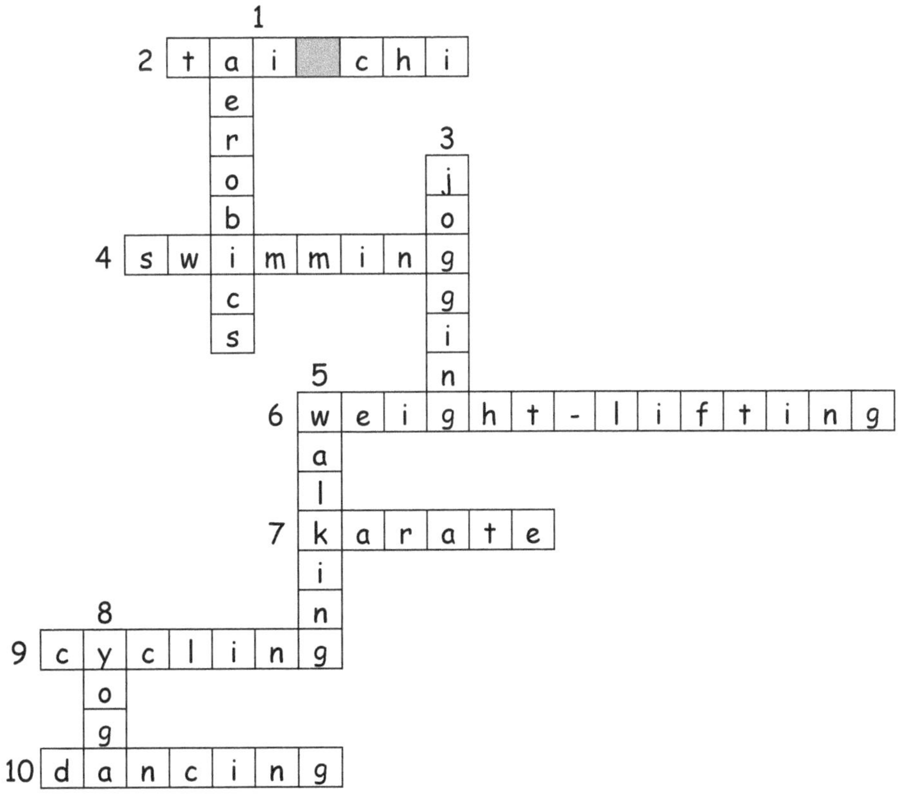

Which Emergency service? page 78

1. Fire.   2. Police.   3. Ambulance.

Emergency services, page 79

1. Fire, please.   2. Ambulance, please.
3. Police, please.   4. Ambulance, please.
5. Police, please.   6. Fire, please.

Shops, page 81

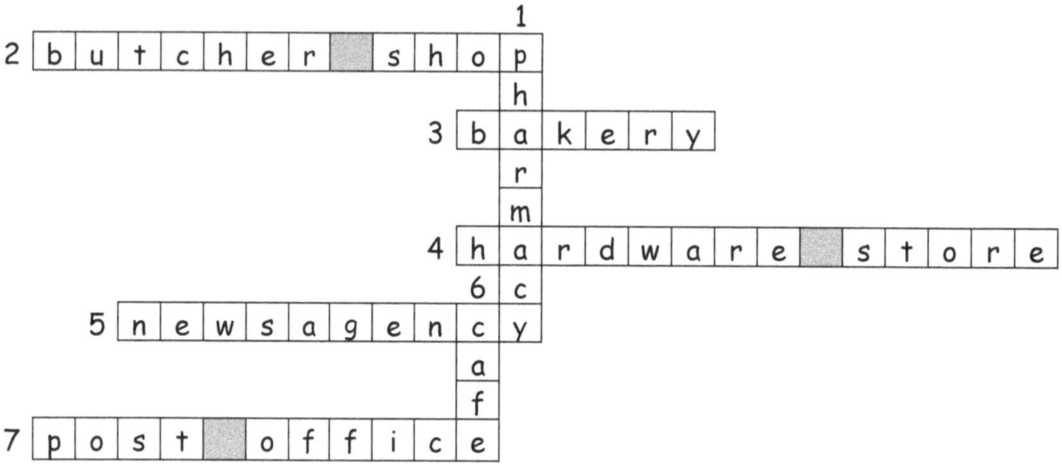

Supermarket words, page 83

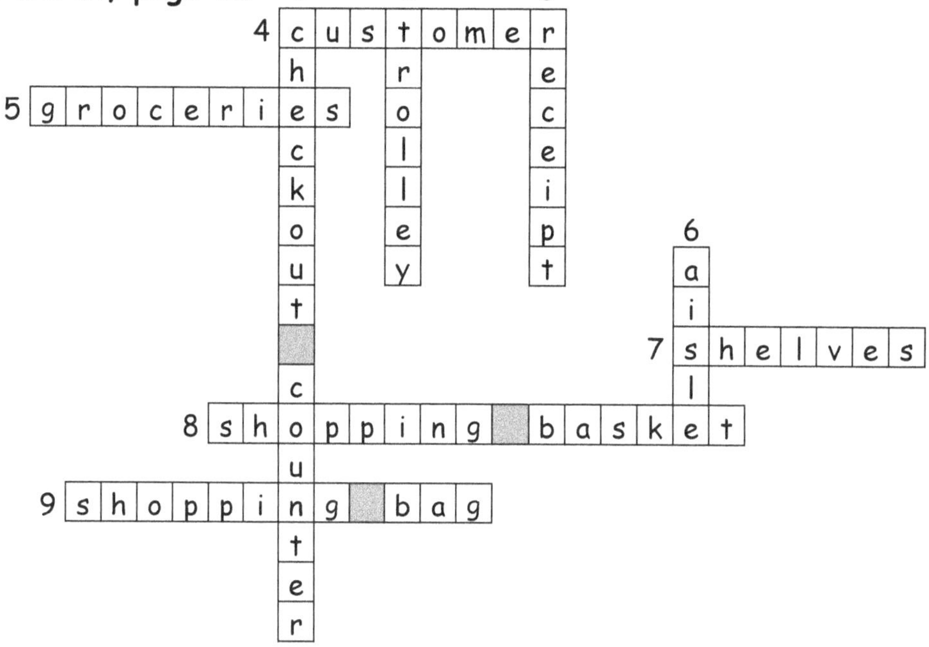

Containers, page 85

1. a can of fish   2. a jar of jam   3. a bottle of oil   4. a bag of nuts
6. a carton of milk   6. a tube of toothpaste   7. a box of washing powder

Containers, page 86

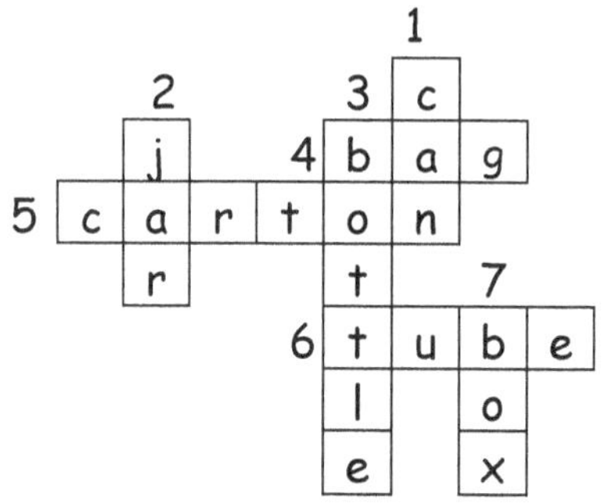

What is in the cupboard? page 87

The tomato soup is **below** the cherries.

The tomato soup is **above** the dog food.

The tomato soup is **next to** the pumpkin soup.

The tomato soup is **between** the pumpkin soup and the vegetable soup.

Buying lunch, page 89

```
          1
      2 s a n d w i c h
        a
        l
3 p i z z a       4         5
        d       b         p
              u         i
      6 f r i e d   r i c e
        r       g
      7 o       e
    8 s a l a d 9 f r u i t
      o
      u
      p
```

At the pharmacy, page 91

```
          1
          m
      2 a p r e s c r i p t i o n
          d
        3 o i n t m e n t
          c
          i       4
          n       s
        5 p e r f u m e
                  n
        6 d r o p s           8
              7 c o s m e t i c s
                  r       a
                  e       b
                  e       l
                  n       e
                          t
                          s
```

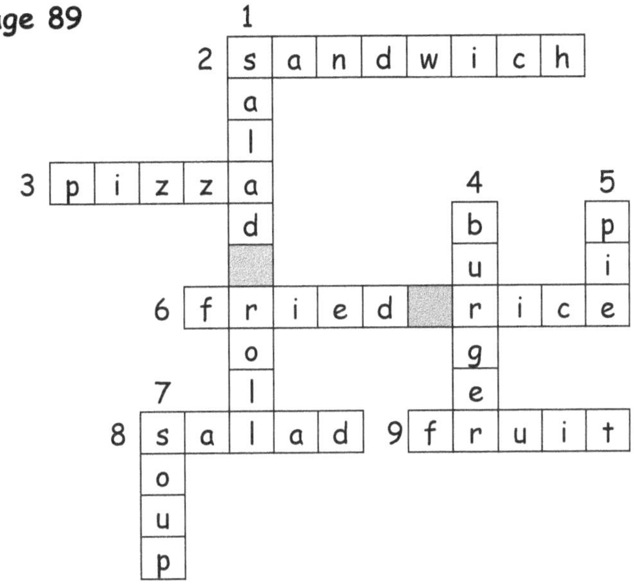

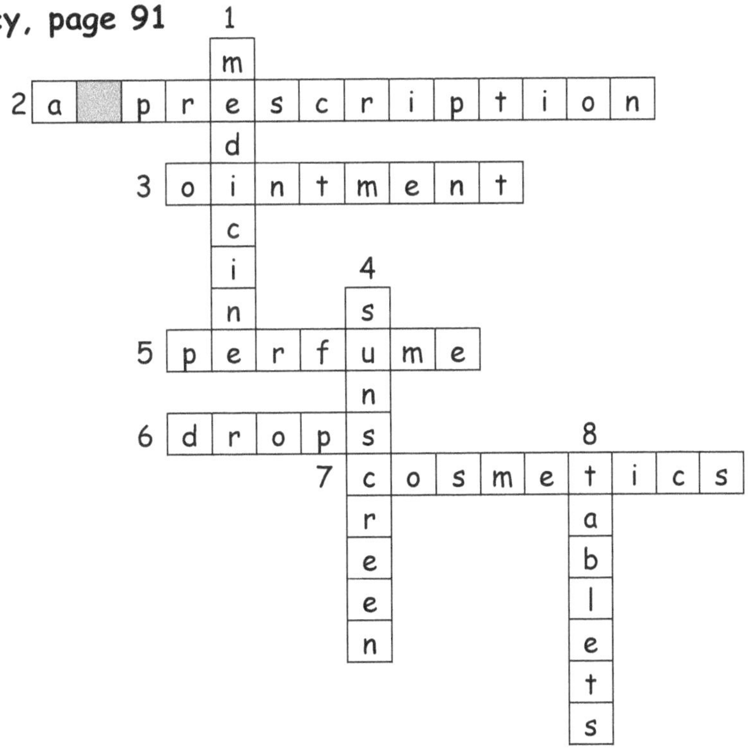

Things in the kitchen, page 93

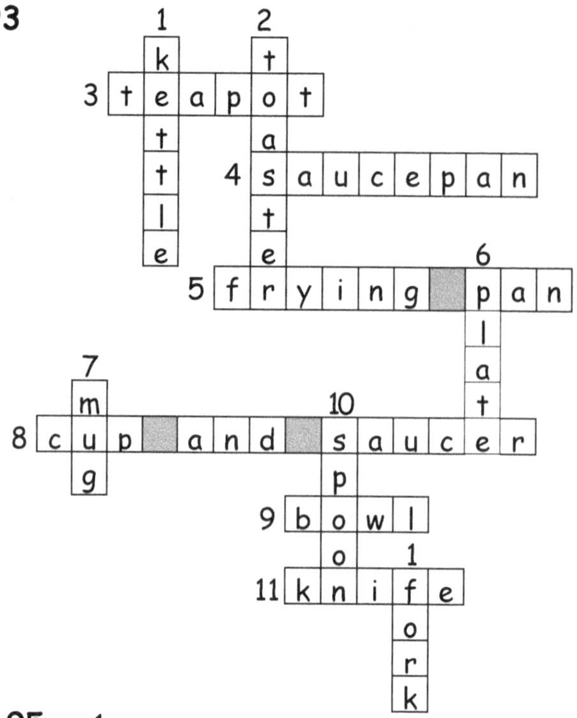

At the electrical store, page 95

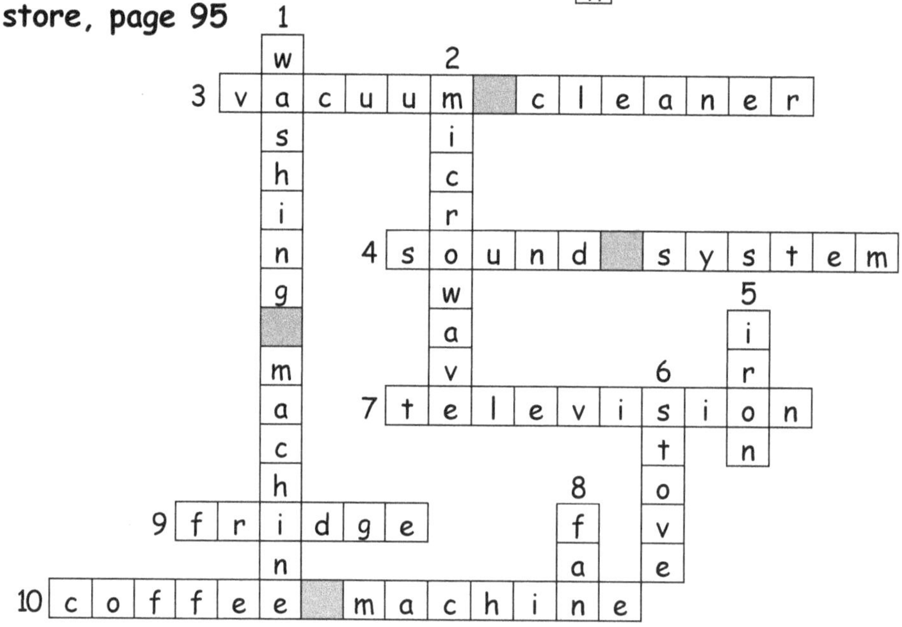

Hardware store, page 97

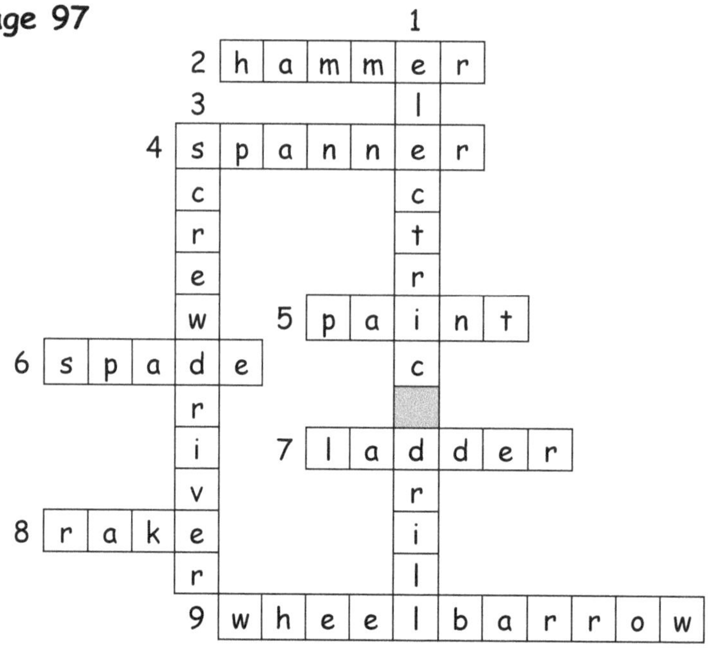

Furniture store, page 99

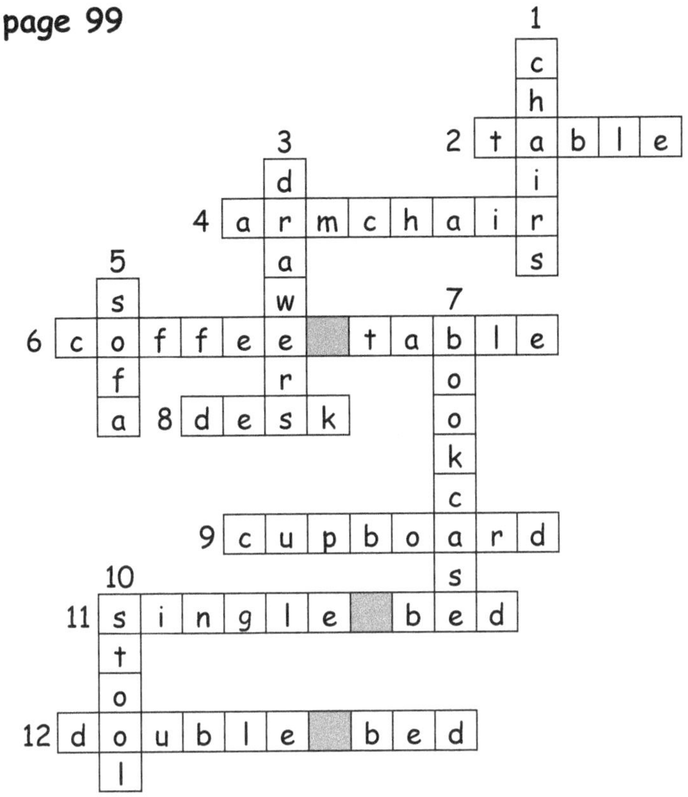

Where can we buy things? page 100

Furniture store	Electrical store
sofa, single bed, table, armchair	washing machine, vacuum cleaner, television, microwave
Hardware store	**Pharmacy**
hammer, paint brushes, ladder, screwdriver	medicine, perfume, prescription, drops

Where can you find things at home? page 101

Kitchen	Bedroom
fridge, toaster, cupboard, kettle, stove, saucepan, microwave	bed, cupboard, drawers
Living room	**Garden**
sofa, coffee table, armchair	rake, spade, wheelbarrow

Transport, page 103

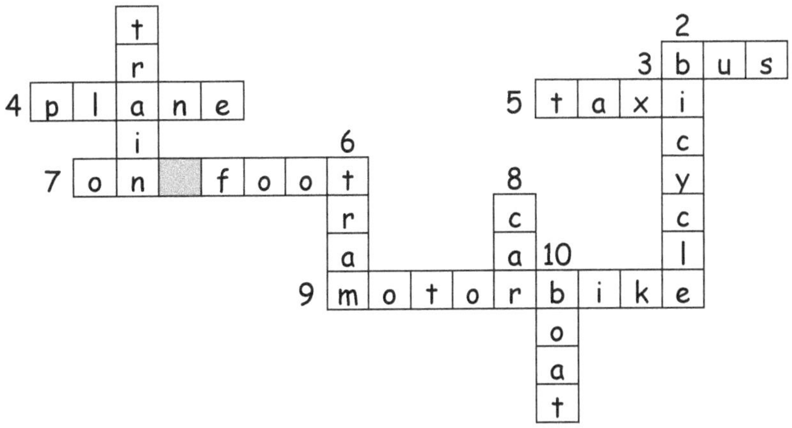

Places, page 105

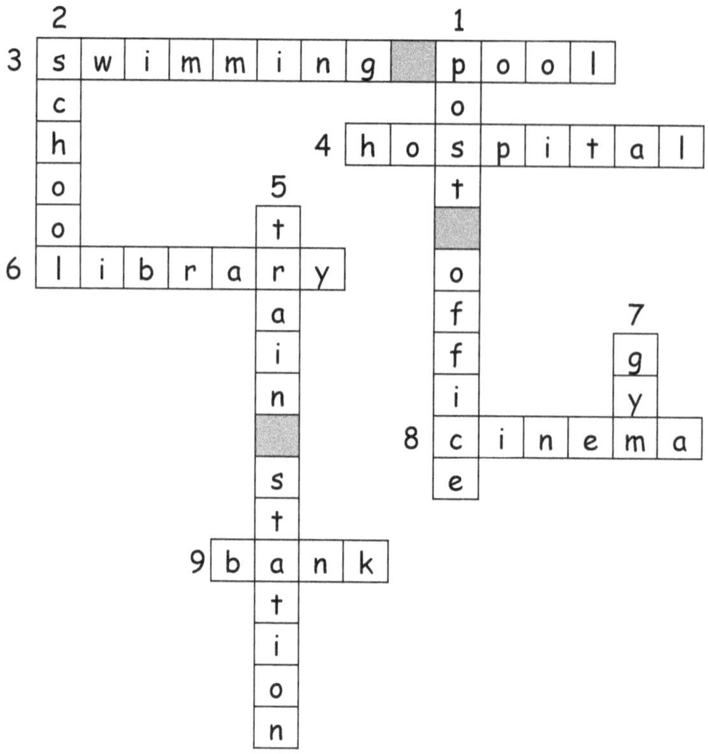

Train Travel, page 106

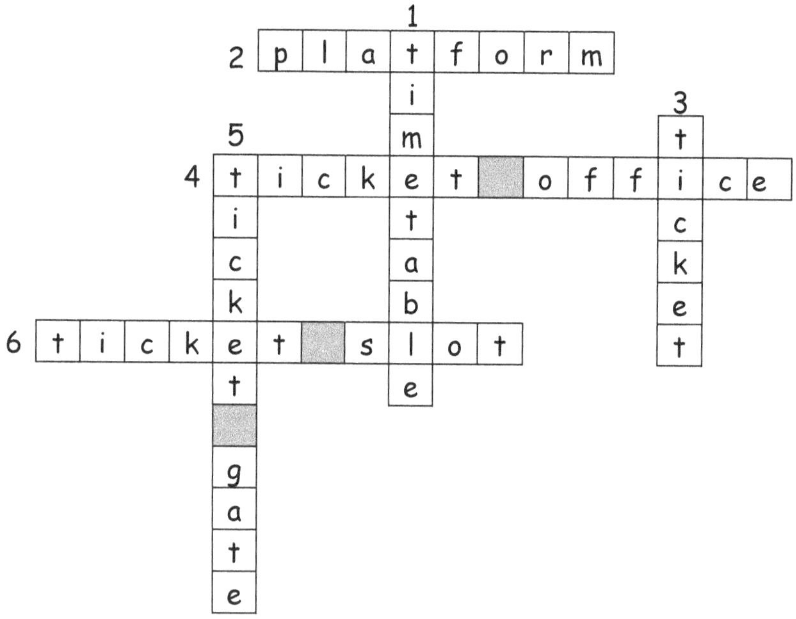

Word lists, page 107

Food	Clothes
strawberries apricots soup rice cheese	shirt coat jeans skirt jacket
Jobs	**Transport**
plumber mechanic nurse painter hairdresser chef	boat motorbike plane train

Boyer Educational Resources books and audio CDs

'Understanding Spoken English' – (books with audio CD) international editions

Reader (A5), Audio CD, Language workbook

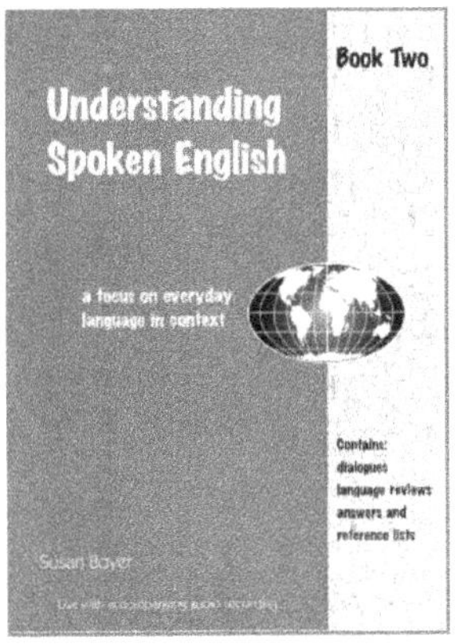

'Understanding Everyday Australian' – series (books with audio CD)

Workbook & Audio CD

Spelling and Pronunciation for English Language Learners

Understanding English Pronunciation

Word Building Activities for beginners of English

English Language Skills Level One

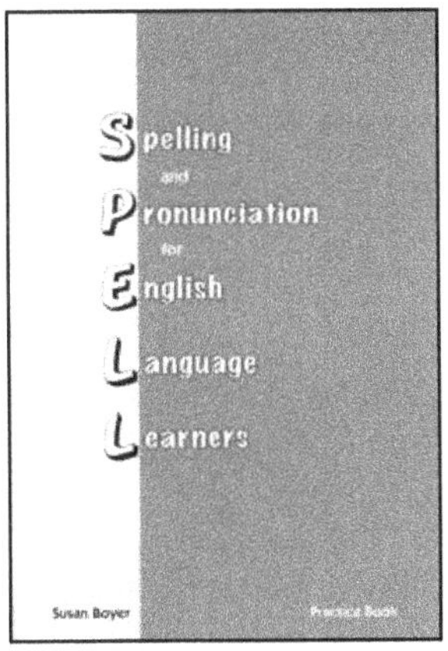

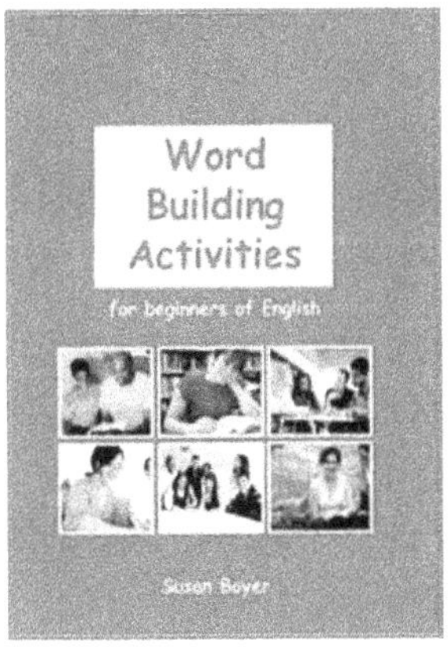

Spiral bound Teacher's Books with photocopiable activities such as surveys, role-cards & vocabulary activities:

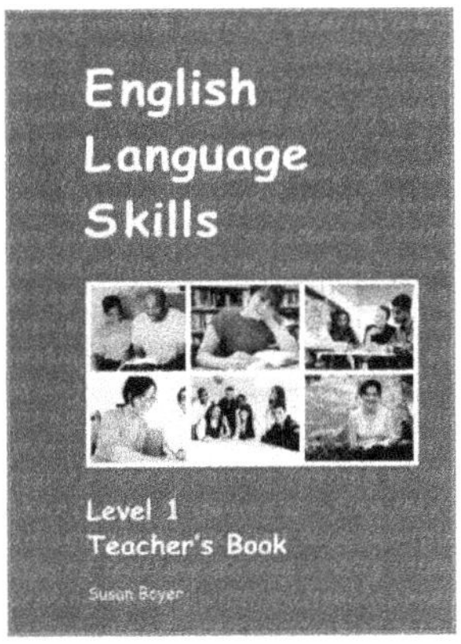

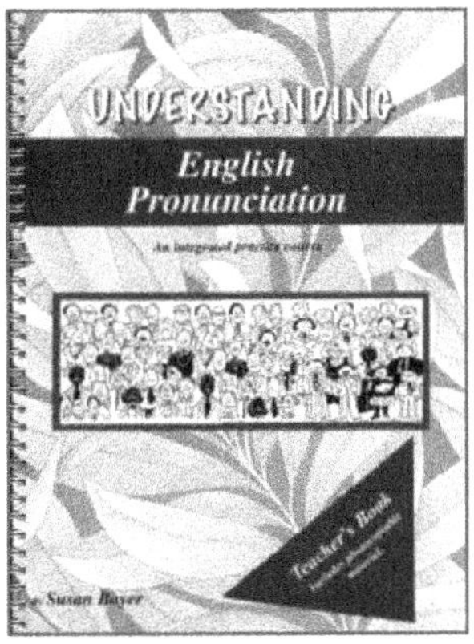

All teacher's books are A4 size. Student's books contain language exercises and answers.

www.boyereducation.com.au

Boyer Educational Resources

Office phone/fax: +61 (0)2 4739 1538 **e-mail: boyer@eftel.net.au**
Websites: www.boyereducation.com.au **www.englishebooks.com**

	Title	ISBN	Price (AUD)
Spelling and Pronunciation	Rhyming Stories - practice with the sounds and spelling of English (A5)	978 1 877074 06 6	$19.95
	Rhyming Stories -audio CD	978 1 877074 37 0	$19.95
	Rhyming Stories - language workbook (A4)	978 1 877074 38 7	$29.95
	English Vowel Sound Spelling Charts A4 Colour (20 reusable charts)	978 1877074 39 4	$29.95
	Phonemic Chart of English Sounds A3 Colour (laminated set of 2)	978 1877074 05 9	$10.95
	Spelling and Pronunciation for English Language Learners	978 1 877074 04 2	$19.95
	Understanding English Pronunciation - Student book only	978 0 958539 57 9	$29.95
	Understanding English Pronunciation - Audio CD (Set of 3)	978 1 877074 03 5	$39.95
	Understanding English Pronunciation - Teacher's Book	978 0 958539 59 3	$44.95
Focus on Australian content	People in Australia's past - audio CD	978 1 877074 35 6	$19.95
	People in Australia's past - language workbook A4	978 1 877074 36 3	$44.95
	Understanding Everyday Australian - Book One	978 0 958539 50 0	$29.95
	Understanding Everyday Australian - Audio CD One	978 1 877074 01 1	$19.95
	Understanding Everyday Australian - Teacher's Book One	978 0 958539 52 4	$44.95
	Understanding Everyday Australian - Book One & Audio CD	**978 1 877074 16 5**	**$39.95**
	Understanding Everyday Australian - Book Two	978 0 958539 53 1	$29.95
	Understanding Everyday Australian - Audio CD Two	978 1 877074 02 8	$19.95
	Understanding Everyday Australian - Teacher's Book Two	978 0 958539 55 5	$44.95
	Understanding Everyday Australian - Book Two & Audio CD Pack	**978 1 877074 17 2**	**$39.95**
	Understanding Everyday Australian - Book Three	978 1 877074 20 2	$29.95
	Understanding Everyday Australian - Audio CD Three	978 1 877074 21 9	$19.95
	Understanding Everyday Australian - Teacher's Book Three	978 1 877074 22 6	$44.95
	Understanding Everyday Australian - Book Three & Audio CD	**978 1 877074 23 3**	**$39.95**
Beginner English	Word Building Activities for Beginners of English	978 1 877074 28 8	$29.95
	English Language Skills - Level One Student's Workbook	978 1 877074 29 5	$19.95
	English Language Skills - Level One Audio CD	978 1 877074 31 8	$19.95
	English Language Skills - Level One Teacher's Book	978 1 877074 32 5	$49.95
	English Language Skills - Level 1 Teacher's Book & Audio CD	978 1 877074 33 2	$59.95
Focus on 'International English'	Understanding Spoken English - Book One	978 1 877074 08 0	$29.95
	Understanding Spoken English - Audio CD One (1)	978 1 877074 10 3	$19.95
	Understanding Spoken English - Teacher's Book One	978 1 877074 11 0	$44.95
	Understanding Spoken English - Book One & Audio CD	**978 1 877074 18 9**	**$39.95**
	Understanding Spoken English - Book Two	978 1 877074 12 7	$29.95
	Understanding Spoken English - Audio CD Two (1)	978 1 877074 14 1	$19.95
	Understanding Spoken English - Teacher's Book Two	978 1 877074 15 8	$44.95
	Understanding Spoken English - Book Two & Audio CD	**978 1 877074 19 6**	**$39.95**
	Understanding Spoken English - Book Three	978 1 877074 24 0	$29.95
	Understanding Spoken English - Audio CD Three	978 1 877074 25 7	$19.95
	Understanding Spoken English - Teacher's Book Three	978 1 877074 26 4	$44.95
	Understanding Spoken English - Book Three & Audio CD	**978 1 877074 27 1**	**$39.95**

www.boyereducation.com.au

www.ingramcontent.com/pod-product-compliance
Lightning Source LLC
Chambersburg PA
CBHW081137090426
42742CB00015BA/2866
* 9 7 8 1 8 7 7 0 7 4 2 8 8 *